Boeing

Philip Birtles

PLYMOUTH PRESS

Ian Allan
PUBLISHING

CONTENTS

Introduction	3
1. The Classics	5
2. 747-400 Development	14
3. Powerplants	27
4. Sales and Service	32
5. Future Developments	73
Appendices	
I. Specification	85
II. Production	86

Front cover: Thai Airways 747-400.
Thai Airways

Back cover: Lufthansa 747-430 D-ABVA
c/n 23816 which first flew on 21 April
1989 was delivered to the airline on
23 May named *Berlin*. *Lufthansa*

First published 2000

ISBN 0 7110 2728 5 (Ian Allan Publishing)

ISBN 1-882663-51-9 (Plymouth Press)

Published by Ian Allan Publishing

an imprint of Ian Allan Publishing Ltd, Terminal House,
Shepperton, Surrey TW17 8AS.

Distributed in the United States of America by Plymouth
Press Ltd, 101 Panton Road, Vergennes, VT 05491.
Call: (800) 477-2398 or (802) 877-2150

Printed by Ian Allan Printing Ltd, Riverdene Business Park,
Hersham, Surrey KT12 4RG.

Code: 0008/C

Previous page: All Nippon Airways ordered six CF6-powered standard 747-400s
initially, later also adding the Domestic version. ANA 747-481 JA8094 (c/n 24801;
l/n 805) was delivered on 28 August 1990. *All Nippon Airways*

Above: A computer-enhanced reproduction of Virgin Atlantic 747-4Q8 G-VFAB
(c/n 24958) in the new colours introduced in 1999. This aircraft was originally
allocated to JAS, but was delivered to Virgin on 28 April 1994 and named *Lady
Penelope*. *Virgin Atlantic*

INTRODUCTION

Above: Privately-owned Asiana operates in competition with state-funded national carrier Korean Air, and ordered four GE CF6-80C2-powered 747-400s in April 1989 for its long-haul routes to Europe and the USA. Asiana 747-48E Combi HL7413 (c/n 25405; l/n 880) was the airline's first delivery, on 1 November 1991, and entered service between Seoul and Los Angeles on 15 November. *Boeing*

When first launched, the original 747 put the entire Boeing company into mortgage, but with profitable production lines building the 707/C-135, 727 and 737 at Renton, there was sufficient cash flow to sustain the programme while the Jumbo Jet began generating revenue.

Now the situation has changed. The 747 has been the largest generator of income for Boeing over the last 30 years and the 747-400 has been the best seller of all. However, the market wants larger-capacity airliners with anything from 500 to 1,000 seats to overcome growing airport congestion, and requires more range, but the airlines are not prepared to spend significantly increased sums for these developments. In addition, it is likely that the introduction will be relatively slow, as the market accepts and uses these enormous airliners, slowing down the return on investment to such an extent that it could be uneconomical for Boeing.

The chapter on the 747-400 development could have been covered in one paragraph with the Performance Improvement Package, but that would not have recognised the enormous amount of engineering and financial resources invested by Boeing in project designs, involving fuselage stretch, wing-root extension, new wing design and a totally-new double-deck airliner.

Although Boeing's total annual turnover is in excess of the gross national product of even quite significant nations, with the production rate of the 747-400 down to possibly nearly one per month in 2000, and heavy investment in the New Generation 737 'Baby Jet', the 757-300 and 767-400ER (neither of which has yet achieved significant sales), and the 777X long-range version, there is little resource left to cope with the massive investment required for a 747-400 development.

Another major change since the launch of the 747 is that there is a significant alternative source of jet airliners with Airbus in Europe, which has now gained a 50% market share and has helped drive down prices and force greater efficiency in production and operation. Although Airbus does not produce a direct competitor to the 747, many of the early Jumbos were bought for range and not capacity, and were therefore flying with empty seats on the long 'thin' routes. Now, with the availability of the A340, this need no longer be the case. In addition, Airbus is seriously planning production of the A3XX to take care of the higher-capacity requirements.

Boeing and the European partners of Airbus, later joined by Airbus Industrie, have undertaken joint studies of the next-generation large airliner, but no agreement has been reached on how to work together. With the investment required it would seem that the most effective way to move forward would be totally international, but the two major airframe producers would have to forget national pride and work out an agreement to design and build an aircraft, and share the market. It will have to be an all-new aircraft, and, by sharing the technology, it will serve the traveller much better, and continue to bring the costs of air travel down in real terms.

Although much has been written about the 747-400, it is believed that this book brings together for the first time the sales and operational history, as well as the continuing saga of 747-400 developments. Much of the preparation for the book involved solitary desk-top research, but the final result would not have been possible without the support of my good friend Bob Hood, the project leader of the Comet restoration team at the Seattle Museum of Flight, who has consistently helped with finding the best contact at Boeing to provide much essential data and illustrations. My good friend Nick Granger has, as always, helped fill in some of the gaps from his comprehensive picture library, while new contacts discovered while compiling this book have included David Riley of Asian Aviation Photography and Gary Tahir in Canada. The collection of photos, often of elusive aircraft, has been one of the major challenges of this book.

Additionally, much help has been received from the airline operators with photos, diagrams and data, including many of the delivery dates. Although the production list has been compiled from a number of sources, the final gaps were filled and authentication was achieved from *Jet Airliner Production List, Volume 1: Boeing* by John Roach and A. B. Eastwood — an excellent compilation.

Finally, my thanks to my wife Martha, who continues to provide enthusiastic support for my aviation writing. She often likens my photograph-taking to fishing; I can wait all day with hardly a bite, but when one comes it is worth the time.

Philip Birtles
Stevenage, Hertfordshire
March 2000

Above: Lufthansa placed an initial order for 10 747-400s, the first delivery being 747-430 D-ABVA (c/n 23816) on 23 May 1989. *Gerd Rebenich/Lufthansa*

1. THE CLASSICS

Above: The Boeing-owned 747 prototype N7470 has been used for a number of development tasks in addition to the original certification programme. In this photo it is fitted with GE CF6-50 turbofans used as an alternative powerplant for the earlier 747s. *Boeing*

For an airliner that made one of the major evolutionary steps in commercial aviation, the first Jumbo Jet started in what may be considered a somewhat casual way with one customer for a programme which was to use much of the vast resources of the Boeing Commercial Airplane Company.

By early 1965 Douglas was proposing a stretched version of the DC-8, carrying initially 259 passengers over ranges of nearly 4,000 miles. Boeing was not keen to stretch the Intercontinental 707 similarly into a 250-seat airliner due to limitations with increasing the height of the landing gear to give adequate clearance against tail strike with a longer fuselage. Juan Trippe, President of Pan Am, was interested in a larger aeroplane altogether, and Charles Lindberg, his technical adviser, suggested that a new airliner might be developed around the new turbofans being designed for the giant USAF C-5A military

transport competition. Boeing had already been studying larger airliners, looking at 250-seat, 300-seat and 350-seat double-deck layouts, but two decks did not gain favour because of difficulties with the emergency evacuation of large numbers of people from the upper deck, and the fact that the lower deck would take up valuable underfloor cargo space, which is a good revenue-earner even if a full load of passengers is not carried.

The logical move was to look at future requirements in air transport and make the bold step into the design of a new wide-body airliner with a capacity of up to 400 passengers. Following a telephone call from Bill Allen, President of Boeing, to Juan Trippe, confirming that Pan Am was serious about buying the new big jet-airliner, preliminary design commenced in the autumn of 1965. The new programme became a fully-fledged new aeroplane programme, led by Mel Stamper, in May 1966,

Above: Pan Am was the original launch customer of the Boeing 747 programme, ordering 25 aircraft in April 1966. Pan Am 747-121 N747PA was the first production aircraft and was delivered to the airline on 3 October 1970. It was retired from service in August 1993 and is now withdrawn from use and stored at Norton AFB in California.
Boeing

with a first flight targeted optimistically for 17 December 1968 — the 65th anniversary of the Wright brothers' first powered flight. Not only were the challenges to design, build and fly the new Jumbo Jet, but also to build a factory large enough to produce the Boeing 747 in large numbers over the coming decades.

Pan Am signed a letter of intent for 25 Boeing 747s in December 1965, specifying a 400-seat airliner with a range of just over 5,000 miles, a take-off capability on a hot day with full load from an 8,000ft runway, and a cruising altitude of 35,000ft. An additional last-minute requirement was that the new airliner should be designed for the provision of the carriage of cargo through a nose loading-door, because Trippe believed that, with the expected entry into service of the supersonic transports within 10 years, the 747s could then be used mostly for air freight. This requirement for the carriage of air cargo greatly influenced the overall design of the 747, including the distinctive cockpit position above the fuselage and the cabin width capable of taking two-abreast cargo containers, each measuring 8sq ft. As a result, sales of all-cargo 747s have been significant over the years, although the Pan Am aircraft remained in the passenger configuration, despite the penalties of higher take-off and landing weights built into the early aircraft to give cargo options.

Pan Am confirmed the launch of the 747 programme by signing a contract in April 1966 for 25 aircraft worth $550 million — the largest single order in value ever placed for an airliner. The order was conditional upon sufficient further orders being placed by other airlines to make the programme a practical proposition, but Boeing had sufficient confidence to commence construction of a new special production facility to maintain the delivery schedules. While Pan Am was to take delivery preference, Trippe was prepared to allow his major competitors, such as Japan Airlines, Air France, BOAC and Alitalia, if they ordered the 747, some early delivery positions, to avoid a possible ban due to suggestions that the aircraft was too noisy, too large, or too heavy.

While the design programme commenced, the major challenge was to create a new manufacturing facility, with about 50 sites considered right across the USA. Site selection had commenced in October 1964 in case Boeing won the C-5A contract, the final choice being made in the following April. The favoured site was to the south of Tacoma in Washington State, adjacent to McChord Air Force Base, but had to be rejected due to the difficulties of land purchase and politics. The eventual selection was at Everett, about 40 miles north of Seattle, where the airport of Paine Field already existed, and where some 700 acres of woodland were

Above: The 747-200 used the experience of the early 747-100s to achieve a better range capability with more powerful engines, and structural improvements allowed a higher take-off weight. Known initially as the 747B, it was designated as the 747-200 and replaced the earlier 747-100s. The first 747B made its maiden flight on 11 October 1970. One of the 747-200's recognition features eventually became its 10 cabin windows on each side of the upper deck, as shown on this United example at the point of takeoff. *United Airlines*

cleared for the new factory, although Boeing purchased around 2,000 acres in all. The far-sighted investment in the additional land has allowed expansion over the years, to triple the production space for the assembly of the Boeing 767 and 777, as well as further major support facilities.

A serious disadvantage of the site was the lack of rail transport access for major components to be delivered, as at that time local roads were inadequate, but Bill Allen was adamant about the site of the new factory. The first priority was to build a five-mile rail spur to the new site, ascending to a height of 500ft above sea level and costing $2 million, its first use being to bring in construction materials to the muddy, rain-soaked site. To maintain the tight production programme, the factory was still being constructed around the workers building the mock-up and setting up the initial jigs, the cost of the initial 200,000,000cu ft structure being $200 million. The new factory was intended only for final assembly of 747s, with sub-assemblies, systems and equipment being supplied from 48 of the 50 states in the USA and 17 foreign countries. Some 50,000 people were initially involved in the 747 programme, designing, producing and

assembling 827,000 parts, as well as constructing the new factory. One of the major sub-contractors was Northrop, which built most of the fuselage, but nose sections were built by Boeing at Wichita. Another major manufacturing facility, both for parts and tooling, was Boeing's Auburn factory, opened in time to participate in the new programme from the start.

Although there were critics of the 747 programme, both for the high business risk and also the possible high loss of life in the event of an accident, the size of the aircraft was justified by the annual growth in 1965 of international passenger traffic by a significant 15%, with domestic travel not far behind. If the size of the new airliner was a risk factor, from an engineering point of view it was a scaled-up 707 using similar structural approaches, and was also powered by four engines, but with greater power. Pan Am believed that it would have the market lead, with an airliner able to carry three times as many passengers as a Boeing 707 and offering the lowest seat-mile costs to date. However, the unexpected economic recession of 1970 created an overcapacity just when the new airliner was entering its revenue-earning career; Pan Am had been keen to maximise capacity, the

Above: The 747SP featured a shorter fuselage and a longer range to allow direct flights of over 5,000 miles on lower-density routes. The first example, N747SP, made its maiden flight on 4 July 1975 and was delivered to Pan Am on 26 April 1976, transferring to United Airlines in February 1986. It was withdrawn from use at Las Vegas in March 1995, and finally broken up at Ardmore a year later. *Boeing*

original Boeing concept having been engineered around a 300-seater similar to the later long-range 747SP which was 48ft shorter than the original 747.

In the early stages, the other major airlines were not enthusiastic about such a large airliner, but the fear of Pan Am dominating the international air routes stimulated many of the international carriers — including loyal Douglas customers — to contact Boeing for details of its new airliner. Many were astounded by the size of not only the new aircraft but also the production facilities. The price of a 747 in 1977 was approximately $21 million, which 20 years later had increased to $107 million.

Safety was paramount in the design and engineering of the 747 to ensure the minimum risk to the large number of passengers to be carried. With loads of between 363 and 490 passengers, special consideration had to be given to loading and unloading techniques. The passenger version has five doors on each side of the cabin, wide enough to allow two people to pass through side-by-side, with inflatable escape slides in the event of an emergency landing on land or water. With a cargo capacity of up to 125 tons, the freighter and convertible versions have an upward-opening nose which permits straight-in loading on the main deck, and a side cargo-door is optional. The 'Combi'

version has a cargo-door on the left-hand side, aft of the wing, to allow mixed loads of passengers and cargo to be carried on the main deck, separated by a removable bulkhead, with room under the floor for baggage and additional cargo. The upward-opening side cargo-door is 11ft 2in wide and 10ft 3in high; in the all-cargo layout, up to 12 pallets or containers can be carried. There is plenty of room in the main deck cabin for a number of seating layouts, from the First class at the front, to twin-aisle 10-abreast seating in high-density economy layouts. Normal flightcrew are a Captain, First Officer and Flight Engineer, with up to 33 cabin attendants to ensure passenger safety and comfort.

There were some 75,000 engineering drawings, and the aircraft needs an acre of parking space at an airport. The fuel capacity, if converted to petrol, would be enough to drive an average car 10,000 miles a year for 70 years, and there is about 135 miles of electrical wiring. To produce the first aircraft to schedule, the design of parts, assemblies, equipment and systems had to be frozen as soon as a configuration was settled upon. Any design changes or refinements would not only increase costs but also bring delays which, if too great, could prompt a decision to cancel the programme, so high were the risks involved; improvements could be built in at a later date.

Above: Boeing 747SP N347SP (c/n 21024; l/n 270) on a test flight prior to delivery to Pan Am as N532PA on 29 March 1976. It was transferred to United in February 1986, becoming N142UA, and was withdrawn from use in July 1994, before being finally scrapped at Ardmore in February 1999. *Boeing*

The first Boeing 747 was finally rolled out on 30 September 1968 — less than three years after Pan Am had signed the letter of intent — by which time orders had been received from 26 airlines. Aircraft No 1, N7470, named City of Everett, was painted mostly white, with a red cheat line. By this time, the programme was costing about $1 million a day, not including the costs of the plant; the final total development was estimated to have reached $1 billion. The maiden flight of this new concept in air transport was made from Everett on 9 February 1969 — just under two months later than the intended (but impossible-to-achieve) date of 17 December 1968. The 747 was trying to meet an unrealistic delivery programme, with only seven months in product development in which to define the aircraft and estimate its weight and performance. It took just 34 months from the launch of the programme to delivery of the first certified 747, and only four years had elapsed between launch and entry into service.

The major problem for the new Jumbo Jet was that it was overweight by 11,000lb, as the Pratt & Whitney JT9D engines developed for the military C-5A had enough power for a 600,000lb aeroplane but not for the 710,000lb 747. The four main undercarriage units, with four wheels on each leg, helped distribute the ground-loading to more acceptable levels, and were steerable to provide ease of ground-handling; the twin-wheel nose leg was located

below the high-mounted cockpit. Weight was increased by the triple-slotted trailing-edge flaps, and full-span leading-edge slats were the only way to maintain a docile slow-speed performance without increasing the wingspan beyond the limits of airport terminal areas and existing maintenance facilities. The initial 747-100 could accommodate up to 66 First class passengers, with 308 in Economy, plus up to 60,000lb of cargo.

The maiden flight was crewed by Jack Waddell, Brien Wygle and Jesse Wallick, and although it was a success, with stick forces as light as the smaller Boeing 727, due to a malfunction the flaps remained down during the entire 45min flight. The wing sweep of 37.5° with a thick root and thin wings achieved Mach 0.9, and cruising altitude was supposed to reach 45,000ft after fuel burn-off, but the increase in overall structural weight, and the poor power of the engines almost caused contract cancellations. Fortunately Pratt & Whitney was able to increase the thrust from under 39,000lb to 43,500lb to help achieve the performance targets, at the same time converting the engine from military standard to a commercial one capable of civil certification and quiet, economical operation.

Another major challenge encountered during early flight-testing was the problem of wing flutter, caused by the suspension of heavy engines on thin wings. The quick fix was to add

Above: A number of the early 747-100s were converted to cargo use, as had been planned by Juan Trippe, the boss of Pan Am, when he placed the original order. Flying Tigers 747-132F N805FT (c/n 20247), seen at London Heathrow in June 1989, was originally delivered to Delta Air Lines as N9900 in November 1971. It was converted to the cargo configuration in June 1977 for Flying Tigers, with an upward-opening cargo-door similar to the Combis and with all the passenger services removed. Flying Tigers merged with FedEx in August 1989 and the aircraft has been operated by American International Airways since June 1994. *Author*

weights to the front end of the outboard engines to provide dynamic balance; the problem was cured on the later, more powerful 747-200 by strengthening the wing structure.

The flight development programme utilised five 747s — the No 1 company-owned aircraft and four production aircraft, later delivered to customers. More than 1,400 hours were flown in 1,013 flights, FAA certification being achieved on 30 December 1969, despite doubts over engine performance. During the 15 months of flight-testing, there were 55 engine changes, which compared poorly with testing of the smaller 737, during which only one engine change had been required. Although alternative engines had been considered from General Electric and Rolls-Royce, the JT9D was the only one which could be ready in time. As part of the development programme, the fourth production 747, N731PA, flew to the Paris Air Show in June 1969. The 5,160-mile flight was made non-stop, demonstrating the long range, despite doubts due to the temperamental engines.

When the 747 commenced commercial operations with Pan Am on 21 January 1970 the problem of excess weight and low-powered engines still remained, and the inaugural flight was delayed by seven hours due to

unserviceability with the first aircraft, which had to be replaced by a second. Engine unreliability caused many delays, bringing criticism not only for Pratt & Whitney, but also Boeing and Pan Am, which at one time had five 747s grounded due to engine problems. In addition, Boeing had a fleet of some 30 engineless 747s parked at Everett waiting for Pratt & Whitney to correct the faults.

Despite the problems and uninformed criticism during the early stages of the programme, the Boeing 747 was found to be easy to handle, particularly in the low-speed regime. High-speed stability was judged excellent, with crosswind landing characteristics as good as — or better than — any airliner in service at the time. Although wake turbulence was expected to be severe, it was found to be little more than experienced with the Boeing 707. Once the powerplant problems had been cured, the overall engineering quality of the original design was demonstrated by the sale of 176 747-100 series, the last of this version being No 601 off the line, delivered to Japan Airlines in November 1984.

On the original 747-100 the space in the hump behind the cockpit was used in some early cases as a crew rest area, as originally planned by Boeing, but it was increasingly adopted as passenger accommodation, particularly for up to 19 Business class passengers. It was reached by a spiral staircase (also used by the flightcrew) located just behind the First class compartment on the main deck. In the early versions, this upper-deck passenger area was often fitted with three windows on each side, but with the development of the improved 747-200 series, the upper deck was fitted with 10 windows on each side. In later 747-300 and -400 versions, the upper deck was further extended to accommodate as many as 99 passengers in an Economy layout, with improved emergency exits.

Although the market predictions for offering the 747 with General Electric CF6 engines were not very encouraging, the decision to offer alternative power was taken by T. Wilson of Boeing during the economic difficulties of 1969-71. It was estimated to cost a further £75 million to re-certificate the 747 with CF6 engines, requiring different support struts, weights, aerodynamics, bypass ratios, air intakes and performance. Following Boeing's decision to offer CF6 engines, nearly 40% of 747 production was so-powered; later, with the sponsorship of BOAC, Rolls-Royce RB211 engines were offered. With the option of CF6 and RB211 power, as well as later-series Pratt & Whitney JT9D engines, Boeing announced in September 1977 the 747-100B, incorporating improvements already adopted in the 747-200 which increased the maximum allowable taxi weight to 753,000lb from 735,000lb. For the Japanese domestic market a special short-range version of the 747-100, the 747SR, was developed with capacity increased to 550 passengers, with fewer toilets and galleys required for the shorter flights. The structure, particularly around the undercarriage, was strengthened to withstand the higher number of take-offs and landings for the given number of flight hours, and gross weight was reduced due to less fuel being required. Japan Airlines introduced this version into service in October 1973 on the Tokyo to Okinawa route.

The 747-200B is dimensionally similar to the 747-100 with the same passenger capacity, the first of this improved version being the 88th aircraft off the line and flying for the first time on 11 October 1970, followed by delivery to Northwest Orient. Originally powered by four P&W JT9D-7R4-62 engines developing 54,750lb thrust, the 747-200B had an increased gross weight of between 775,000 and 820,000lb. To cope with this increased weight there was additional structural reinforcement, and it was not long before the CF6-50E, developing 50,100lb thrust, and the RB211-524-02, with 51,600lb thrust, were also available. On 12 November 1970 a 747-200B set a new world heavyweight record during tests, by taking off at a gross weight of 820,700lb, and during testing with RB211 engines the gross weight take-off was increased to a record 840,500lb on 1 November 1976. The typical range of the 747-200B with 442 passengers and baggage at a gross weight of 820,000lb is 6,440 miles. The 747-200B was certificated on 23 December 1970; as with the 747-100, a Combi version was produced, with the first delivery made to Air Canada in February 1975.

The 747-200C is a factory-built fully-convertible version which can be configured for all-passengers, all-cargo, or a combination load with the passengers ahead of the cargo. The cargo distribution system is built into the floor, and the passenger flooring is loaded above the cargo rollers. The first example of this version flew on 23 March 1973, with certification on 24 April and delivery to World Airways on 30 April. The 747-200F is the dedicated specialist cargo version of the aircraft, with an upward-opening nose, and all windows and passenger services deleted. The cabin can accommodate two rows of containers 8ft wide and 8ft high, with the length going up to 40ft to maintain interchangeability with use by rail and road transport. In addition to the opening nose, the 747-200F can also be fitted with an upward-opening door on the port side of the fuselage, aft of the wing, as with the Combis, giving a 10ft headroom in the rear part of the cabin. Some 250,000lb of main-deck cargo can be loaded by two people in 30 minutes. Certification was achieved on 7 March 1972, the first delivery being of D-ABYE to Lufthansa on 10 March.

Above: As well as new-build 747-200Fs, some passenger aircraft were converted to the full cargo configuration including the upward-opening nose loading-door. Japan Airlines 747-221F JA8165 (c/n 21743) was originally delivered to Pan Am on 25 July 1979 as N904PA and was acquired by JAL in 1983. The aircraft is seen visiting London Heathrow in June 1989. *Author*

In competition with the smaller Lockheed TriStar and McDonnell Douglas DC-10, Boeing had looked at a completely new trijet configuration while the 747 prototype was under construction, but soon rejected the idea due to lack of airline interest. What did evolve, however, was the 48ft 4in-shorter, approximately 300-seat 747SP (for Special Performance), with range increased to over 7,600 miles. Pan Am had been considering the DC-10, but the 747SP fitted its requirement while maintaining crew and maintenance commonality, and the airline ordered 10 of the ultra-long-range aircraft. Before the availability of computers and fly-by-wire, Boeing was able to offer a pair of airliners with identical handling qualities, avoiding crew conversion from one version to the other.

The 747SP had to be capable of flying non-stop from New York to Tokyo against a 25kt headwind, requiring reductions in weight while retaining airframe strength. Simpler, lighter flaps were part of the weight reduction, 1,800lb being saved by the time the first aircraft was ready for flight. The 747SP had reduced passenger-mile costs on long-range flights, the seating being for up to 28 First class passengers and 271 Economy on the main

deck and 32 more on the upper deck. Fuel capacity was increased to 50,359gal US, and gross weight was reduced to between 630,000 and 700,000lb.

The 747SP gained certification on 4 February 1976 and entered service with Pan Am in April 1976 on the New York to Tokyo service, soon achieving a daily utilisation of 14.1hr. In 1986, when Pan Am was experiencing financial difficulties, the trans-Pacific routes were sold to United, which took over the Pan Am 747SP fleet. However, on a special charter flight in January 1988, a 747SP operated by Pan Am flew around the world in three stages, with a flying time of 39hr 26min and an elapsed time of 46hr 26min.

The next major development was the 747-300, which is easily recognisable by a major rearward extension of the upper-deck fairing to accommodate up to 91 Economy class passengers. A conversion of existing 747-200s is also available to bring them up to the 747-300 standard. Flight-testing commenced with the JT9D-7R4-62-powered version on 5 October 1982, and this was joined by a CF6-50E2 in December. Certification was achieved on 7 March 1983, with Swissair being the first airline to put this version into service

Above: El Al Cargo Airlines 747-258C Convertible 4X-AXD (c/n 21190) was delivered to the airline on 31 December 1975 and is seen ready for departure at London Heathrow in October 1987. *Author*

Above: Featuring the extended upper deck later adopted for the 747-400, 747-357 Combi HB-IGD (c/n 22705) was delivered to Swissair on 5 March 1983 and is seen on turnaround at Zurich in August 1983. This aircraft was withdrawn from use and stored at Marana in September 1999. *Author*

on 28 March. As with the earlier models, Combi and convertible versions were also available. The aircraft can carry typically 496 passengers, but Japan Airlines' high-density, short-range domestic 747-300SR can take a maximum of 630. Gross weight is between 775,000lb and 833,000lb, and range is 7,710 miles.

With the development of the 747-400, the earlier versions became known as the 747 Classics.

2. 747-400 DEVELOPMENT

Although the 747-400 was treated as a progressive development of the 747-300, incorporating 1980s technology in a 1960s airframe with structural improvements, Boeing freely admits that it would never want a repeat of the problems caused by the new programme. So great were the difficulties that, when it began the design and development of the Boeing 777, the company went through a complete cultural change involving design/build teams to ensure that whatever was designed could be effectively produced, and using the principle of customer as partner, not only internally, but externally, to ensure the resulting product was what the market wanted.

Boeing announced the development of the 747-400 in May 1985, using new technology conservatively, since any changes had to be justified on cost benefit grounds. This new version replaced all the previous versions of the 747, the final -200F (the 393rd series -200 off the Everett production line) being delivered to Nippon Air Cargo of Japan in November 1991. This marked the end of a 21-year production run including 205 -100s, 45 747SPs, 223 all-passenger -200s, 78 Combis, 73 freighters, 13 convertibles, 81 -300s, four USAF E-4Bs and two US Presidential aircraft.

In establishing the overall requirements for the new version, Boeing consulted 14 major international airlines, including Northwest, Singapore Airlines, British Airways, QANTAS, Cathay Pacific, KLM and Lufthansa. Boeing wanted to go for a minimum-change aircraft, particularly on the flightdeck, where the analogue instruments were to be retained. This was supported by Cathay, one of the launch customers, in order to minimise retraining.

However, there was strong pressure from the other potential launch customers to update the flightdeck, since they were experiencing the advantages of the 757/767 entry into service and the advanced flightdecks of the Airbus family, which provided greater reliability, improved information when required, and saved the cost and space of the third crew member. Digital avionics had advanced through about three generations in capability since the first

Above: One of the major changes adopted for the 747-400 was an advanced two-pilot flightdeck with side-by-side CRT displays. The two EICAS displays are located centrally in front of the thrust levers. The Captain's PFD screen on the left provides flight operations information, and the ND screen is used for navigational data. *Boeing*

analogue 747, which did not have the capability of making automatic landings in poor weather. The new features which could be adopted with the use of digital avionics included collision avoidance, datalink with the ground base ensuring up-to-date status reports, wind shear warnings and 4D navigation, as well as such accepted facilities as autoland.

With the airlines' demand for modern technology, the new 747-400 cockpit was to have a similar layout to the already-developed two-crew flightdecks for the twin-engine 757/767 programme. However, having experienced even greater advances with the Airbus A320 which was just entering service, the airlines wanted even more sophistication, with the displays side-by-side instead of one above the other, and various features added. Individually the requested changes were not difficult, but when all were combined in the software programmes for the onboard computers the incorporation became difficult. The 747-400 central computer is linked to every major system in the aircraft, and trying to integrate all the individual systems computers while retaining compatibility became a massive problem. The hydraulic system is virtually unchanged from earlier versions, apart from refinements to match the new design. Working pressure is maintained at the traditional 3,000lb/sq in. Electrical supply is provided from four engine-driven 90kVa Sundstrand generators with back-up from the auxiliary power unit (APU) in the event of failure, and the digital database wiring and circuit breakers are reduced significantly from earlier 747s. Fuel management and measurement is fully automatic.

The 747-400 was offered from the start with the choice of three engine types, all requiring different installation and engineering, giving different performance both in thrust and economy, and all three requiring certification with the airframe. The engines available are the P&W PW4056, the GE CF6-80C2 and the R-R RB211-524G/H, all in the 60,000lb (270kN) thrust range and fitted in nacelles interchangeable with the 767's. All three engine types have achieved a high level of reliability over many years of commercial service, at the

same time competing to provide the greatest power for the best fuel economy. All three turbofans have reduced fuel-burn by between 5% and 10% over the previous decade, and all are capable of full-authority digital engine control (FADEC). The other major source of installed power was the all-new Pratt & Whitney Canada PW901A APU, located in the extreme rear of the fuselage, which first ran on test in 1987. This burns 40% less fuel than the previous versions while working more effectively and environmentally friendlily. It has fully-automatic start, monitoring and shut-down, driving two generators for operation in the air or on the ground.

In the first year there were 18 different customers making their individual demands on an inexperienced workforce. However, once the problems with the 747-400 flightdeck were resolved, it formed the basis of the architecture of the later 777 programme. Depending upon which engines are fitted, the gross weight of the 747-400 varies from 800,000 to 850,000lb, with an option available for up to 870,000lb. With its additional fuel, reduced drag and more fuel-efficient engines, the 747-400 has a range of up to 8,400 miles. To help prove the capability of the new PW4000-series engines, the first 747-400 set a new weight record by reaching an altitude of 2,000m after taking off at a gross weight of 892,450lb.

The flightdeck was changed from a three-person layout to one operated by two crew, although for the longer flights a second crew is carried due to one team exceeding their duty time. There is, therefore, provision for crew rest areas. Usually the Captain and First Officer who are in command for the departure have a rest for a few hours during the cruise in the middle of the flight, and return to the flightdeck for the latter part of the flight and arrival at the destination. The switch from three to two crew also involved a change from analogue electro-mechanical instruments to full digital cathode-ray-tube displays. The systems displays, previously the responsibility of the Flight Engineer, are located in the cockpit roof between the pilots, and any problems are highlighted by the Engine Indication & Crew Alerting System (EICAS). This not only gives

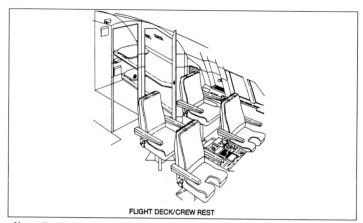

Above: The Boeing 747-400 flightdeck is operated by two pilots, with a pair of additional non-operating crew seats behind. At the rear of the flightdeck is a crew rest area, for the longer flights where one crew would run out of duty time. *Boeing*

warnings of faults, but also provides the crew with corrective actions.

The cockpit differences are so great that crews flying the earlier versions have to undertake comprehensive training before being allowed to operate the new version, although the transition has not proved too demanding. The converting pilots learn quickly to change scan and cues in the roomier flightdeck, to which the most common reaction is: 'How did we manage in the past?' The two crew are kept informed of flight and systems operation with six 8in x 8in (200mm x 200mm) cathode-ray tubes (CRTs). One pair is dedicated to flight control functions, another pair to navigation and the third to EICAS. The flight control and navigation screens are placed side-by-side. The Captain's left-hand primary flight display (PFD) screen shows horizon, attitude, airspeed, altitude, vertical speed and heading. The Captain's right-hand navigation display (ND) screen replaces the old moving map, and with the aircraft symbol located in the centre of the display the pilot can view all around while in a busy terminal area. The ND has four alternative modes covering approach, VOR (VHF omni-directional range), map and flight plan, either with a full compass rose or a selected enlarged quadrant. Full-colour weather-radar pictures

can be superimposed to warn of hazardous weather conditions. The screens are reversed for the First Officer. If a PFD fails, the information can be immediately switched to the ND panel, with the other pair still operating. Basic electro-mechanical instruments are fitted as a back-up, in the unlikely event of failure of all the flight and navigation displays.

The EICAS screens are used for the checklist functions for the various stages of operation, and are programmed to provide the crew only with the information required for that stage of operation, cutting out unnecessary data. The two EICAS screens are positioned in the centre of the flightdeck, one above the other. The top screen is usually used to display primary engine data, together with aircraft status information. The lower screen also presents engine data and systems pages. Should a fault occur, a warning or caution alerts the crew, who refer to the quick-reference checklists to follow the correct procedures. Each system has redundancy built in to survive multiple failures, providing the necessary actions are taken. This not only covers safe operation of the aircraft, but facilitates despatch. As a result, the number of instruments, switches and warning lights is reduced dramatically, from 971 on analogue flightdecks to 365 on the 747-400. The aim

improvement is digital
engine control, known as
'power-by-wire'.

The 747-400 was not
just a new flightdeck. In
addition to incorporating
new technology from the
systems developed in the
757/767 programme,
there was a requirement
for an increase in range.
Wingspan was increased
by 6ft with the addition of
drag-reducing upward-
swept 6ft-high winglets
— which are the major

was to reduce workload to between a half and
one third of that on the earlier 747s, justifying
the removal of the Flight Engineer. The EICAS
screen gives systems status, and schematics
(systems diagrams) can be called up by the
crew at any time on any of the CRTs. Another

recognition feature of this version — and
weight was reduced by 6,000lb through the use
of new lighter, high-strength aluminium alloys
in the structure. A further 1,800lb was saved by
fitting carbon brakes in place of steel units, and
new wider wheels with low-profile tyres to

maintain the overall diameter.
The increased span and
carbon-fibre winglets resulted
in an increase in the aspect
ratio of the wing, reducing
induced drag and giving a 3%
improvement in range, along
with enhanced cruise
performance. The addition of
3,300gal US of fuel in the

Left: A major external
recognition feature of the
747-400 are the
composite, upward-
swept, 6ft-high winglets
located on the increased-
span wings. *Lufthansa*

Above: The 747-400 had weight reduced by the introduction of carbon brakes and new wider wheels with reduced-profile tyres. The main undercarriage consists of four steerable units, each with four wheels; shown is the starboard wing-mounted unit, with the right fuselage unit beyond. *Lufthansa*

Above: The nose undercarriage unit is a conventional twin-wheel steerable unit. That fitted to BA 747-436 G-BNLW is being checked before departure on a flight to Singapore and Sydney. *Author*

tailplane gave a further range increase of 400 miles. In practical terms, this means that the 747-400 can fly direct from London to Singapore and Hong Kong, whereas the 747-200s usually had to make refuelling stops in the Middle East, Karachi or Delhi.

The launch of the 747-400 in 1985 revitalised sales of the 747, which were beginning to slow down with more modern airliners becoming available. As a result of the development of the new version, sales practically doubled, ensuring Boeing's dominance of the large jet-airliner market at least up to the end of the century. Boeing's aim was to produce a derivative of the 747-300, using the latest available technology,

Above: Access to the forward underfloor cargo-hold is via an upward-opening door under the front cabin. *Author*

Above: Baggage and freight is loaded in containers into the rear underfloor cargo-hold. *Author*

consistent with an economic payback. In addition to the incorporation of new technology in the systems, the cabin was completely redesigned to give an even wider look, with new galleys, toilets, overhead bins, air-conditioning and cabin services. The overhead bins more than doubled in volume, taking the most stubborn carry-on bag. The main deck can take 3-4-3-abreast seating with twin 20in aisles and more than adequate headroom of 110in. The cabin trim and furnishings had to comply with the latest fireworthiness standards, and the seat structure is designed to withstand forces of up to 16g, which is approaching the limit of human endurance. To improve air circulation in the cabin, the air-conditioning zones have been increased from three to five, with a higher ventilation rate. There is plumbing for up to 26 toilet positions within the cabin.

The airlines' requirement was for an increase in range of 1,000nm, which was met partly by reducing the fuel-burn by as much as 37% compared with the first 747-100s. Another target was to reduce operating costs by 10%.

In addition to the use of new aluminium alloys in major structural areas to reduce weight and improve corrosion protection, lightweight composite materials developed in the 757/767 programme were used in a number of non-structural areas, including the winglets. An additional leading-edge slat was added to the wing, and drag was further reduced by re-contouring the wing-to-fuselage fairing. With the wingspan increased to a nominal 211ft, when the full load of fuel is taken on, the bending moment causes the winglets to move outwards by 1ft, extending the span on the ground to 213ft. The basic design suffered testing incidents, although never a catastrophic total structural failure. In the new model, all areas which had been prone to cracking in the past were strengthened, the large front end having thicker frames, skins and doublers to avoid the previously expensive repair schemes. Corrosion protection was further improved by the use of white epoxy paint in the underfloor areas, particularly those below the toilets and galleys. The 747-400 economic design life was set at 60,000hr, 20,000 flights or 20 years. Many of the earlier 747s have exceeded 60,000 flying hours, and are continuing in service with regular monitoring of the structure to ensure its integrity is maintained.

As part of the improved systems, a digital central maintenance computer (CMC) was installed, with access on the flightdeck to determine fault analysis and correction at an appropriate time. The CMC displays are located on the central console between the two pilots, co-ordinating built-in test equipment (Bite) interpretation of all systems centrally, and recording faults in plain English on the screen. Not only does this assist with any unserviceability, but it allows planned maintenance 'on condition', avoiding unnecessary breakdowns. The digital database replaces miles of wiring, increasing reliability and reducing weight. The Honeywell (Sperry)

flight-management computer (FMC) can not only compute direction and timing by the use of inertial navigation, but, allowing for progressive fuel-burn, can predict the operational altitude at various stages of the flight, bringing 4D navigation and assisting with the air traffic control. The FMC takes a maximum of 3sec to complete a normal calculation, which takes up to 20sec in earlier versions of the 747.

The Collins autopilot hardware is basically the same as that installed in the 757 and 767, but is loaded with new software. An important new facility on this fully-digital Triplex system for the 747-400 is Altitude Intervention, which can compute unexpected operational changes in en-route altitude at the request of Air Traffic, without the crew having to recalculate the flight plan. There was a smooth introduction of the 747-400 to Cat IIIB Autoland, giving a zero decision-height and a visibility of 75m for all-weather landings. Should there be an engine failure on the approach, the autopilot automatically deflects the rudder to compensate. New rudder actuators decrease the runway minimum control speed by 10kt, and for better control the rudder has an increase of 5° of movement (to 30°) over earlier models of the 747.

It was not just customer demands for the flight-deck systems which caused Boeing so many problems with the 747-400, but also the new interior, which was totally redesigned with all-new panels, shapes and materials. On a new aircraft programme, this would all have been allowed for, but the drastic changes simply were not taken into account in what was originally regarded as a mere derivative. The first flight was delayed by over a month due to these and other difficulties, but by 1989 the bulk of the problems had been solved, the 747-400 in due course becoming the best-selling variant.

As with the previous versions, the new variant was also adapted to Combis, high-density domestic versions without winglets for the Japanese market, and freighters with a carrying capacity of up to 124 tons of cargo, which was up to 26 tons more than the -200F. The 747-400 domestic version for Japan Airlines and All Nippon Airways has the same

Above: The cabin interior of the 747-400 was completely redesigned to give an even wider look and features larger overhead bins to take even the most stubborn carry-on bag. The cabin width allowed for a maximum of 343 seats in Economy, but Cathay configures its aircraft at 242 with miniature TV screens in the seat-backs as part of the passenger entertainment system. *Cathay Pacific*

wingspan as the 747-300, but, once a critical number of cycles has been reached on the short, high-density routes, the aircraft are reconfigured with 747-400 wingtip extensions and winglets for the less structurally-demanding international operations. The cargo version retained all the external features of the -400, except that the upper deck stayed at the shorter length as used on the 747-100 and -200, since there was no need for the additional capacity above the main deck.

The lead aircraft in the flight development programme was P&W PW4056-powered, the second aircraft GE CF6-80C2-powered, and the third had R-R RB211-524G engines, as adopted by British Airways. The basic price of the aircraft was in the region of $120 million.

The first 747-400 was rolled out at Everett in late January 1988, the first 737-400 having been rolled out at the narrow-body plant at Renton, east of Seattle, the same morning. Orders for the 747-400 then stood at 117 aircraft, with options on a further 54 from a total of 17 airlines. These launch orders were worth in excess of $12 billion, the launch customer being Northwest with orders for 10 aircraft powered by the Pratt & Whitney

engines. The first 747-400 made its maiden flight from Paine Field on 29 April 1988, delayed by some six weeks due to late deliveries by some Boeing suppliers and difficulties with integration of the new electronic systems. The maiden flight lasted for 2hr 26min, and a speed of Mach 0.7 and altitude of 20,000ft were reached. The second aircraft to join the flight development programme was powered by the GE CF6-80C2 engines. Rolls-Royce gained a Certificate of Airworthiness from the British CAA for the 58,000lb-thrust RB211-524G on 25 March 1988. This was in time for the first set to be shipped to Boeing for installation in the third 747-400, which joined the flight development programme on 28 August in the colours of Cathay Pacific, which was the launch customer for this version.

By October 1988 Boeing was admitting delays to the programme due to receiving more orders than expected, the customer configuration variations, and the certification with three different engines. British Airways and QANTAS had elected for identical specifications to allow flexible usage of the combined fleets when appropriate, and to help reduce costs. To

Above: New galleys have been installed in the 747-400, including the spacious one at the rear of the Economy passenger cabin. *Lufthansa*

make up time, aircraft were being flight-tested seven days a week, the aim being to achieve certification and first deliveries by the end of the year. Although other aircraft were also late in joining the flight development programme, the absence of any significant problems during testing helped partly to catch up with the overall schedule. The test aircraft were averaging 65 flying hours a month, with a peak of 90 hours a month early in the programme. All the data collected had to be processed to determine the results, involving a massive amount of analysis. The aerodynamic testing of the increase in wingspan and the winglets, as well as the balance of the new tailplane fuel tank, went smoothly, and by early October 1988 a major part of the flight development concentrated on the digital avionics and refinement of computer software.

By the middle of October, four aircraft were participating in the test activity, with more than 500 flight hours logged in 180 flights. Flutter clearance had been achieved and the performance evaluation of all three engine types had been completed, with fuel economy still to be established. Testing then moved on to low-speed aerodynamic performance and autopilot development, leading to Autoland trials. Handling qualities were equal to, or better than, earlier versions of the 747. During the

flight development programme, amongst the major milestones achieved was a non-stop flight of 14hr duration, and a new world-record take-off weight of a civil aircraft at 892,450lb. Other work undertaken during flight-testing was the compilation of the aircraft flight manuals and the gathering of data for flight-simulator use.

FAA certification was awarded to the Pratt & Whitney-powered 747-400 on 9 January 1989, a month later than originally planned. Had the aircraft been treated more as a new type, rather than as a derivative, targets may have been set at more realistic levels. The eight-and-a-half-month test programme using four aircraft had taken 2,600hr, of which about half were in the air. Certification work continued on the GE and R-R engine versions, the CF6-powered combination achieving FAA certification in May 1989. The RB211-powered version gained a CAA type certificate in June 1989.

European certification was awarded on condition that Boeing complied within two years with full European Joint Airworthiness Regulations (JARs) in respect of upper-deck floor strength and venting in the event of a major cabin decompression. However, there were problems in May with achieving JAR certification for the first GE-powered 747-400 for KLM — not because of the engines, but because the upper-deck floor structure did not meet damage-tolerance criteria caused by differential pressure in the event of a sudden cabin decompression. All the control cables and wiring from the cockpit are located under the upper-deck cabin floor, and any collapse of the floor could be disastrous. As noted previously, Boeing had regarded the 747-400 as a derivative of the earlier 747-300, and therefore not needing to comply with new regulations. The JAR committee defined the aircraft as a new type, due to the large numbers of expected sales and the projected service-life of 30 years. Delay to the delivery of the first aircraft to KLM was avoided by the issue of a temporary JAR Certificate of Validation for 90 days to give Boeing time to provide a solution. Three days after the arrival of the first KLM aircraft on 7 June 1989, Lufthansa received its first 747-400, which was operated under the same temporary conditions. The 90 days were

allowed for negotiation between the JAR and FAA authorities, but since it would take longer to design, produce and embody the modifications, a further extension would be required. By October, agreement had been reached between Boeing and the JAR authorities whereby all 747-400s delivered to European airlines from January 1992 onwards would incorporate the upper-deck modifications, and for those aircraft delivered earlier, the modifications would be available for retrofitting three months after delivery of each aircraft. Rather than provide additional structural strengthening, the lighter and lower-cost alternative was to fit extra venting flaps in the floor, and re-route some of the cables and wiring.

In earlier versions of the 747 the structure around the forward fuselage, known as Section 41, had been prone to fatigue; through the use of modern aluminium alloys the problem was eliminated. This was confirmed by an

Above: The extended upper passenger deck, based on that of the 747-300, is often configured in a Business class layout. In the case of Air Canada it is four-abreast, divided into two cabins. *Air Canada*

Above: The cargo version of the 747-400 retains all the external features of the passenger version, but lacks the upper-deck extension. One of the major operators of this version has been Cargolux. *RollsRoyce*

Above: The PW4056-powered first 747-400 N401PW made its maiden flight from Paine Field at Everett on 29 April 1988, some six weeks later than planned. *Boeing*

accelerated fatigue-test programme on the fuselage, and, although the airframe was designed for a 20,000-cycle life, the test specimen passed 54,000 pressurisations without any major problems.

Although the first production -400 was painted in Boeing colours for the flight development programme, there was never any intention that the company should retain this aircraft, and on completion of the test programme it was refurbished and delivered to Northwest Airlines. The first delivery was made to Northwest on 26 January 1989, within one month of the originally-planned schedule. Total deliveries for the first year were planned to cover 57 aircraft, with the production rate more than doubling to 4.75 aircraft a month. The Boeing 747-400 was ready to earn its keep.

Above: The 20th anniversary of the first flight of the original 747 was celebrated on 30 September 1988 with a flypast in close formation of the Boeing-owned prototype and the first 747-400 over the city of Seattle. *Boeing*

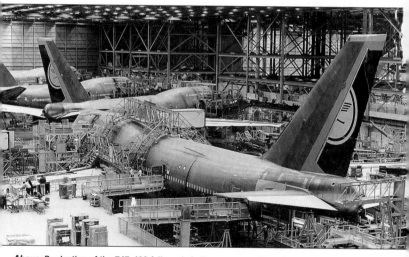

Above: Production of the 747-400 followed similar processes to earlier versions, and initially -400s were built alongside the last of the 747-200s and -300s. The aircraft are assembled surrounded by a large dock for ease of access, and are then moved forward for equipping. The rudders are generally painted before fitting, for balancing purposes. This example is a Combi for Lufthansa, with the rear cargo-door installed. *Lufthansa*

Above: Once the 747-400 is structurally complete it is moved forward in the assembly hall for equipping. The aircraft shown in the equipping stage is the 75th 747 for Japan Airlines, JA8081 (c/n 25064; l/n 851), which was delivered on 13 May 1991. *Boeing*

Above: Following assembly and equipping, aircraft are positioned in a computer-controlled paint-shop for the application of the airline livery, and then pulled out to take a place on the flight line for systems-checking and test-flying. *Lufthansa*

3. POWERPLANTS

As already discussed, the 747-400, like earlier versions of the 747, was offered with a choice of three engine types. These turbofans were all well-established derivatives of earlier service-proven types, and offered increased thrust with better fuel economy and reliability. Each engine type had a common installation with the Boeing 767-300ER twin-jet airliner.

Northwest Airlines, the launch customer for the 747-400, selected the Pratt & Whitney PW4000 series, which is a third-generation two-shaft turbofan for widebody civil and military transports. During initial testing in April 1984, the first engine achieved 61,800lb (275kN) of thrust, and the engine started flight testing on an Airbus A300B on 31 July 1985. Certification was achieved in July 1985 for an initial power of 56,000lb (249kN) as the PW4056, with service entry on a Pan Am A310

on 20 June 1987, followed by the PW4060 of 60,000lb (267kN) in 1988. (The last two digits of the engine designation indicate the power, the initial PW4056 engine developing 56,000lb thrust and the PW4060 60,000lb.)

The PW4000-series engine incorporates single-crystal turbine blades with aerodynamically-enhanced aerofoils. The fan is single-stage with a titanium ring retaining 38 titanium-alloy blades with aft part-span shrouds. The fan diameter is 93.6in (2.377m) and the initial PW4056 had a bypass ratio of 4.85, a fan pressure ratio of 1:7 and a mass flow of 1,705lb (773kg). The low-pressure (LP) compressor has four stages, with controlled-diffusion aerofoils. The LP turbine has four stages with active clearance control. The high-pressure (HP) compressor has 11 stages, with the first four rows featuring variable vanes.

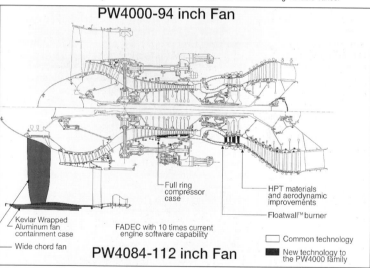

Above: The Pratt & Whitney PW4000 94in fan engine covers the 52,000 to 62,000lb thrust range, achieves a 99.9% despatch reliability and has over 30 million hours of service. To date, 65 airlines use the standard PW4000 turbofans to power their wide-bodied aircraft fleets, with over 60% operating on ETOPS routes with approval for 180 minutes. Development continues using enhancements derived from the later PW4000 100in-fan and PW4084 112in-fan engines. *Pratt & Whitney*

Clearance control is achieved by rotor-case thermal matching. Overall pressure ratio at 56,000lb is 30:1. The HP pressure ratio is increased by 10%, and the HP rotor operates at a 27% greater speed. The HP turbine has two stages, with air-cooled blades cast as single-crystal in the first row and directional-crystal in the second row, retained by a double-hub nickel-alloy rotor with active clearance control. The annular combustors are forged nickel-alloy roll-ring with double-pass cooling and 24 air-blast anti-coking injectors.

With a reduction in parts of around 50% there is a significant improvement in maintenance costs of about 25%. Compared to the JT9D-7R4 used in the earlier versions of the 747, the PW4000 uses 7% less fuel, as well as achieving lower emissions. It was also the first full-authority digital-engine-control (FADEC) engine to be approved for 180min extended-range twin-engine operations (ETOPS), which, although not required for the four-engine 747, demonstrated improved reliability. Like the airframe, the PW4000 engine programme is multi-national, with risk-sharing partners, as well as sub-contractors; participants include Techspace Aero in Belgium, FiatAvio in Italy, Norsk Jet Motors in Norway, and Eldim in the Netherlands, with Asian partners Kawasaki and Mitsubishi in Japan, Samsung in South Korea, and Singapore Aircraft Industries.

Following the PW4056 and subsequent PW4060, a later development was the 62,000lb (276 kN)-thrust PW4062, also common to the 767-300ER.

General Electric announced the development of the CF6 series of turbofan engines on 11 September 1967 for the planned wide-body transports, and the CF6-6D for the McDonnell Douglas DC-10-10 was launched on 25 April 1968.

The CF6-80C2 engine was a major redesign, with higher thrust and improved efficiency, based on the CF6-80A1/A3 but with a 93in (2.362mm)-diameter fan. It has a four-stage LP compressor, with the LP turbine redesigned aerodynamically with 5½ stages. The first CF6-80C2 ran in the test cell in May 1982, later exceeding 62,000lb (276kN) thrust, and was flight-tested on an Airbus A300 between August

and December 1984, achieving certification on 28 June 1985.

As with the PW4000 series, the CF6-80C2 was also produced by an international agreement including SNECMA of France, MTU in Germany, Volvo Flygmotor of Sweden and FiatAvio in Italy.

The main improvements over earlier versions of the CF6 engines included a single-stage fan with the integrally-mounted four-stage LP compressor. Construction is mainly from titanium except for a steel mid-fan shaft, aluminium spinner fairing and a blade-containment shroud consisting of layers of Kevlar around an aluminium case. The 80 composite guide-vanes are canted for improved efficiency. The bypass ratio is 5.05, and the mass flow is 1,769lb (802kg). The LP compressor has the blades and vanes mounted orthogonally, with a dovetail offset from the centre of pressure to reduce bending. The LP turbine has five stages, with cambered struts in the rear frame to reduce exit swirl, which in effect produces another half-stage. The rear hub is heated by exhaust gas to reduce thermal stress. The HP compressor has 14 stages with variable-incidence guide-vanes and, on the first five, stator rows. The blades in the first five stages are made from titanium and in rows 6 to 14 are produced in steel. All the vanes are made from steel. The one-piece steel casing has insulated aft stages. The overall pressure ratio is 30.4 and the core airflow is 340lb (154kg). The two-stage HP turbine casing has active and passive clearance control. The annular combustors are of rolled-ring construction and are aft-mounted with film cooling.

The CF6 used to power the 747-400 is the 56,900lb (253kN) CF6-80C2B1F, which is a unique powerplant/airframe combination.

The Rolls-Royce RB211 is a family of high-bypass and high-pressure-ratio three-shaft turbofans developing a range of thrust from 37,400lb (166.4kN) to over 100,000lb (445kN). Also derived from the basic engine are the RB211-535 and Trent, Rolls-Royce retaining full responsibility for all applications of the complete propulsion system. The original RB211-22B was produced for the Lockheed

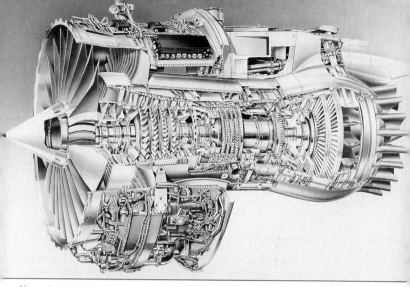

Above: The Rolls-Royce RB211-524G/H-T is the current version of the turbofan for the 747-400. It incorporates the advanced Trent 700 core, improving efficiency and reliability, while reducing maintenance. The RB211-524G/H has been chosen by Air New Zealand, BA, Cargolux, Cathay Pacific, QANTAS and South African Airways.
Rolls-Royce

Left The RB211-524G/H-T turbofans built at Derby are rigorously tested before achieving certification for flight. The environmental testing includes spraying water at a running engine to ensure it continues operating in the most difficult conditions.
Rolls-Royce

TriStar, achieving CAA certification in February 1972 followed by FAA approval two months later. Over 670 RB211-22Bs had been produced when production ceased in 1982.

The RB211-524 series was developed from the RB211-22B, and covered power outputs from 50,000lb (222.5kN) to 60,600lb (270kN) thrust. The RB211-524 entered airline service in 1977, fitted both to the TriStar and the Boeing 747-200.

The RB211-524G incorporates a number of advanced features proven with the smaller RB211-524E4 engine, including a wide-chord fan, 3D aerodynamics, directionally-solidified HP and IP (intermediate-pressure) turbine blades, and an integrated mixer nozzle. Another new feature was the addition of FADEC. The engine can operate at the G rating of 58,000lb (258kN) or the H rating of 60,600lb (270kN), these being mechanically identical, and both power the 747-400 and the 767-300ER which has a 180min ETOPS clearance. The more powerful RB211-524H entered service with the 747-400 in February 1990.

The RB211-524H has a single-stage overhung fan with composite nosecone and 24 hollow wide-chord titanium blades driven by the LP turbine with controlled-diffusion-outlet guide-vanes. The aluminium casing has an Armco containment ring. The bypass ratio is 4.3 and mass flow 1,604lb (728kg). The IP compressor has seven stages and is driven by the IP turbine. Two drums, one of titanium discs and the other of welded steel discs, are bolted together to form one rotor carrying titanium blades. The aluminium and steel casings carry steel stator blades and there are single-stage titanium variable-inlet guide-vanes. The single-stage IP turbine has directionally-solidified nickel-alloy rotor blades which are fir-tree-mounted in a nickel-alloy disc.

The six-stage HP compressor is driven by a single-stage HP turbine, which also has directionally-solidified nickel-alloy rotor blades fir-tree-mounted in a nickel-alloy disc. The HP compressor has welded titanium discs, a single steel disc and welded nickel-alloy discs bolted together as mounts for titanium, steel and nickel-alloy blades. The steel casing carries steel and nimonic stator blades. The three-

stage LP turbine has nickel-alloy rotor blades fir-tree-mounted into steel discs. The fully-annular combustion chambers have steel outer casings with nickel-alloy combustors. Downstream fuel is injected by 18 airspray burners by annular atomisers, and there are high-energy igniter plugs in numbers 8 and 12 burners. The integrated exhaust nozzle has a deep-chute forced mixer. Lubrication is by a continuous-circulation dry-sump system, supplying oil to four bearing chambers with a combination of ball and roller bearings. A 27-litre oil-tank is integral with the gearbox. The accessories, including the integrated-drive generator and aircraft hydraulic pumps, are radial-driven from the HP shaft to a gearbox on the fan casing.

As part of the in-service product improvement, in mid-1996 Rolls-Royce was preparing to test a production RB211-524G/H fitted with the high-compression system of the Trent 700. The requirement was to improve fuel consumption and extend engine component life of what was known as a hybrid demonstrator, but these developments would only be adopted if definite benefits were achieved. By early 1997 a number of operators were concerned about reliability and performance shortfalls with the RB211-524G and -524H engines in service, which were estimated to have cost the airlines $200 million in additional maintenance and operational expenses. Engines were being removed for overhaul after 1,400 cycles (rather than the 2,000+ cycles of competing engines) due to turbine-blade failures, and inadequate exhaust-gas margins meant that maximum thrust was not available at hot and high airfields. Fuel consumption was also higher than anticipated.

The hybrid programme, which was expected to overcome these problems, achieved test-cell certification in April 1997 ready for flight-testing to commence in January 1998. British Airways signed a letter of intent (LoI) with R-R in April 1997 specifying RB211-524HT turbofans for 14 747-400s ordered in September of the previous year, although no decision was made on a retrofit of the remainder of the fleet until October 1998. The flight-testing was expected to take an aircraft out of service for at least six

Above: It is essential that turbofans are fully accessible for routine turnaround maintenance before the aircraft leaves on another service. The RB211-524G/H-T engines fitted to this SAA 747-400 have all the accessories available for inspection from ground level. *Rolls-Royce*

weeks, which would cause a capacity problem for a potential customer airline. However, when Cathay decided to retro-fit the hybrid modifications to its entire fleet of 21 747-400s, agreement was reached to use a Cathay -400 for flight development, followed by a BA aircraft. With the thrust ratings remaining the same, a mixture of engines on individual aircraft would be acceptable, allowing Cathay to carry out a phased programme of updates between 1998 and 2002. Improvements included a 2% reduction in fuel consumption, higher turbine gas temperature margins and a 90kg weight saving for each engine, as well as better reliability. SAA also selected the upgrade in August 1997, and flight-testing began on a BA aircraft with Boeing in November 1997, with certification in January 1998 and service entry on 23 April with Cathay. After this successful entry into service, Rolls-Royce discontinued production of the older versions of the RB211-524G/H engines in favour of the new -524HT.

All three powerplant options therefore produce similar power ratings, and are sold competitively for economic benefits and high guaranteed reliability. In the past, engine manufacturers often enjoyed exclusive supply for aircraft types and gained much of the profit from after-sales support. The increased competitiveness has made purchase prices keener, and the improved reliability demanded by the airlines has reduced earning potential from ongoing support. Engines are now generally modular, allowing easier maintenance; the basic core of the powerplant can be left on the aircraft wing while replacement modules are fitted, thus reducing aircraft downtime to a minimum.

4. SALES AND SERVICE

Above: After completing the flight development programme, the first 747-400 — the 696th 747 to be built — was refurbished and delivered to launch customer Northwest as N661US on 8 December 1989. It is seen here at Sydney in September 1992.
Andrew Briggs

The 747-400 programme was formally launched by Northwest Airlines in October 1985 with an order for 10 PW4000-powered aircraft. Other airlines taking advantage of launch positions were British Airways (BA) with 16 RB211-powered 747-400s plus options on a further 12 aircraft, Singapore Airlines (SIA) which bought an initial batch of 14 PW4056-powered aircraft and six options, Lufthansa with 10 CF6-80C2-engined -400s and nine options, Korean Air with three firm orders and three options, Cathay Pacific with its first two Rolls-Royce-powered -400s plus seven options, and UTA with two GE-powered aircraft. The 747-400M, the Combi version of the -400, was launched into production by an order from KLM for four CF6-80C2-powered aircraft in April 1986, with deliveries starting in February 1989, in addition to four passenger versions.

In the second year after the formal launch, total orders were received for 93 747-400s, with 54 options, new customers being CAAC of China with three Combis, China Airlines (CAL) of Taiwan with five P&W-powered -400s, QANTAS with four RB211-powered aircraft and options

on a further 15, Thai Airways with two plus two, and United, a long-term operator of Boeing airliners, with an initial order for 15 P&W-powered aircraft.

By the middle of 1988, firm orders for the 747-400, including Combis, had reached 146 aircraft. New customers included Air France with 16 CF6-80C2-powered -400s, Japan Airlines (JAL) with 20 CF6-80C2-powered 747-400s and two more for the Japanese Government, Air New Zealand with one R-R powered -400, Malaysian Airlines (MAS) with two GE-powered Combis and International Leasing & Finance Corporation (ILFC) with four aircraft. BA had taken up one of its options, Korean Air increased its order to nine aircraft including two Combis and had selected the PW4000 turbofans, while Lufthansa had specified three Combis within its initial order.

New orders during the latter half of 1988 included Air Canada with three Combis, two more R-R-powered -400s for Air New Zealand, six CF6-powered 747-400s for All Nippon Airways (ANA), and three CF6-powered aircraft for Canadian Airlines. Lufthansa confirmed its options on a further five aircraft (of which one

Above: BA was an early customer for the 747-400, already having been a major operator of the 747-100 and -200. Boeing 747436 G-BNLX (c/n 25435; l/n 908) was delivered on 3 April 1992 and is seen after landing at Sydney in September of that year.
Andrew Briggs

Above: China Airlines, of Taiwan, placed an order in the second year after the launch for five 747-400s. Boeing 747-409 B-164 (c/n 24312; l/n 954) was delivered on 11 January 1993, and is seen at Hong Kong Kai Tak in November 1995.
Asian Aviation Photography

23 May, and Cathay Pacific the first to have the Rolls-Royce RB211 aircraft, with the first handover on 8 June. Lufthansa expected six of its order of 15 747-400s to be in service by the end of the year, and was training the crews, with 180 pilots expected to have completed by July. To help build up crew experience, Lufthansa kept one 747-400 on the high-cycle European routes, and converted crews from the earlier 747s, DC-10s and Airbus A310s.

was a Combi), MAS added four passenger versions to its Combi order and QANTAS doubled its order by adding four 747-400s.

Boeing led all the other commercial airliner manufacturers following a record sales year in 1988. From a world total of 1,121 new jet airliners, the lead Boeing product was the 757, with the 747 attracting 49 orders, all but six being for the 747-400. By this time, 21 airlines had ordered a total of 169 of the latest version of the Jumbo Jet. Also announced in January 1989 was an additional order from MAS for three 747-400s with options on three more, worth around $423 million, with deliveries of the GE-powered aircraft due to start in April 1991. MAS had still to decide whether it wanted an all-passenger version, Combi, or all-cargo.

With the Pratt & Whitney-powered 747-400 certificated by the FAA on 9 January 1989, the first aircraft was delivered to Northwest Airlines on 26 January, initially operating on domestic sectors to gain experience, before being allocated to trans-Pacific routes. Lufthansa was the first airline to receive the General Electric-powered versions with its initial delivery on

Boeing reviewed the production rate of the 747, this rising from 24 aircraft delivered in 1988 to 57 in 1989 — more than doubling, to an average of 4.75 per month. From the experience gained from the delays with the 747-400, due to the problems explained in Chapter 2, Boeing decided to limit the number of configuration options available to customers, since the engineering man-hours required to produce all the alterations increased pressure not only on the 747 programme, but also on the 737, 757 and 767 programmes.

The largest order to date for the 747-400 was placed by All Nippon in February 1989 for 20 aircraft worth some $3.15 billion, in addition to the order for six aircraft placed in 1988. The engine selected was the GE CF6-80C2SF; aircraft deliveries were scheduled to start in 1992. In March 1989 Singapore Airlines (SIA) took delivery of its first two 747-400s, introducing them initially on the regional routes to Hong Kong, Taipei, Tokyo and Perth. In April, QANTAS confirmed two of its outstanding options, taking firm orders for the 747-400 to 10, with 22 options remaining. As with the remainder of the fleet, power was to come from Rolls-Royce RB211-524G engines, and the aircraft were due for delivery in September and November 1990. Also in April, Asiana signed a letter of intent for four -400s, later confirmed as Combis, with the first to be delivered in late 1991. In May, South African Airways (SAA) placed an order for two 747-400s with options on two more, worth $256 million, to be powered by Rolls-Royce engines.

Also in May 1989, Japan Airlines announced its plan to specify two domestic versions of the 747-400 as part of its already-announced order for 20 aircraft. The domestic version would have the undercarriage and fuselage strengthened to cope with the more frequent cycles, and the wing would be the same as the 747-300 without winglets and increased span. The rear fuselage fuel-tank would be deleted, and the aircraft would be configured for 568 passengers instead of around 400 in the normal -400.

Cathay Pacific needed more power from the engines of its 747-400s due to the particular operating conditions at Hong Kong Kai Tak, with its 11,130ft runway and demanding take-off over the city when the wind was coming from the north. It was preferable to take-off out to sea with a tailwind of 7kt rather than head in the other direction, but this also required superior performance from the engines. Boeing was originally offering a 56,000lb-thrust engine, but Cathay needed 58,000lb thrust, and Rolls-Royce produced the RB211-524G. By the time BA placed its initial order for the 747-400, R-R had reached over 60,000lb thrust with the RB211-524H engine, which was also adopted by Cathay after the first two -524G-powered aircraft were delivered; these were later converted to -524H power. Cathay had 24 747-400s on order, all scheduled for delivery by 1995. The early 747-400 deliveries were used on non-stop services to European destinations, with the aircraft delivered after 1991 allocated to Pacific routes to Vancouver, Los Angeles and Toronto, with Chicago as an option. The 747s spend about 14 hours per day flying on these routes, arriving at Hong Kong in the morning, but not departing on the next long-haul flight until

late evening. During the day, therefore, the aircraft are used on high-density regional routes including those to Taipei, Tokyo, Osaka, Singapore, Manila and Bangkok, where the 400 seats are an advantage; this arrangement also avoids the difficulty obtaining sufficient slots for greater numbers of smaller aircraft.

In June 1989 the first 747-400 of 19 for British Airways (G-BNLA) was ready to start crew training at Seattle in preparation for the inaugural flight on 27 July — the 40th anniversary of the first flight of the Comet, the world's first jet airliner. Regular commercial services started on 29 July to Pittsburgh and Philadelphia, allowing crew experience to build up before starting the ultra-long-haul routes. The one-stop service to Australia via Singapore was planned to start at the end of August.

When Lufthansa exercised options on three GE-powered 747-400s in mid-1989 to bring its total order to 18, GE claimed the lead in engines for the -400, with CF6-80 engines specified for 101 aircraft — more than twice as many as either of the competing R-R and P&W engines. Initial deliveries were made to KLM in May 1989 and Korean Air in June.

SIA needed to be able to operate the 747-400 non-stop from Singapore to London with a 44-tonne payload. However, the first three -400s delivered did not have the full performance specification from the PW4000 engines, although this was corrected by the fourth delivery. Apart from this, the introduction went very smoothly, with any in-service problems being with secondary items like the passenger entertainment and environmental systems. The new aircraft was found to be more stable, even at 40,000ft, and the new two-pilot flightdeck was much more efficient, avoiding mental calculations and rule of thumb. The overhead panel contained simplified, automated 'dark, quiet principle' controls for the systems previously monitored by the Flight Engineer. The fuel system was much simplified, with switch-on at the start of the flight with the total fuel-load set, allowing the fuel-flow to be automatically programmed. Pressurisation control on descent is automatic as soon as the destination designator is entered into the FMC. To ensure the flightcrew remain alert throughout

Above: Since ordering four RollsRoyce-powered 747-400s in 1987, QANTAS has progressively increased its long-haul fleet. A QANTAS 747-400 is seen flying over the famous Sydney landmark of the Harbour Bridge. *QANTAS*

Above: Thai Airways placed an initial order for two 747-400s and 747-4D7 HS-TGH (c/n 24458) was delivered on 21 February 1990. *Thai Airways International*

Above: Japan Airlines is the largest 747 operator, using the standard -400 aircraft for long-haul flights and an adapted version for domestic services. JAL 747-446 JA8902 (c/n 26344) was delivered on 19 August 1992, and is seen on final approach to London Heathrow in June 1997. *Author*

Above: At about the time that JAL placed its initial order for 747-400s, the Japanese Government ordered two for VIP and humanitarian flights. Carrying the flight-test registration N6055X, this 747-47C (c/n 24730) was delivered on 17 September 1991 as JA8092; it later became 201101. *Boeing*

Above: With a growing need for air transport and modernisation of equipment in China, CAAC ordered 747-400s on behalf of Air China. Boeing 747-4J6 B2443 (c/n 25881) was delivered on 24 February 1993, and is seen on final approach to Hong Kong Kai Tak in April 1998. Author

the flight, cabin crew are instructed to enter the flightdeck every 45 minutes to offer refreshments, whether requested or not. A second crew is carried for the long flights between Singapore and London, the crew who commanded the take-off making the landing at the destination. The extra crew fly the aircraft for five to six hours during the middle of the flight, while the others are able to retire to the two-bunk air-conditioned rest area. The quickest crews to convert to the new -400s were those used to the cathode-ray-tube (CRT) cockpits of the A310 and 757, while those taking longest had flown only the older 747s introduced before the advent of CRT-flightdeck airliners.

During the delivery flight of the first 747-400 (VH-OJA) for QANTAS, the aircraft was flown from London to Sydney non-stop, arriving at its destination on 17 August 1989. The 20hr 9min flight covered 9,720 nautical miles (18,001km), the aircraft landing with four tonnes of fuel remaining from the total of 183.5 tonnes at take-off. The R-R-powered aircraft carried 18 people including the crew of four QANTAS pilots and one Boeing, with a fully-furnished interior but reduced galley equipment. The fuel used was a special high-density Shell Jet A1, and the aircraft was towed to the end of the runway at Heathrow before engine start to conserve fuel. The QANTAS flight challenged the non-stop UK-Sydney record by an RAF Vulcan from Scampton to RAAF Richmond. The Vulcan was

six minutes quicker, but was flight-refuelled four times.

As with other versions of the 747, a number of options were available, including Combi and Freighter. The CF6-80C2-powered 747-400F was launched in September 1989 with an order from Air France for five aircraft worth $600 million to be delivered from August 1993, complementing the 10 747-200Fs already in service. The 747-400F had undercarriage and wing-skins strengthened to cope with the increased all-up weight, passenger services and windows deleted, and the top cabin extension behind the flightdeck reduced in length similar to the earlier 747-200/-100s. Loading was by an upward-opening nose-door, allowing cargo to be pushed straight in. It retained the extended wingspan and winglets of the passenger -400. With the engines rated at 57,900lb (257kN) take-off thrust, the new aircraft was able to carry 44,000lb (19,954kg) more payload than previous 747 Freighters. Cathay followed in October with an order for two RB211-powered -400Fs and two options, with deliveries of the firm orders planned for mid-1994 and October 1995. By the end of September 1989 there were 20 747-400 Combi models on order for six airlines, KLM having been the launch customer.

In October, Northwest announced orders for 46 airliners from Boeing, with options on a further 44. Included were six additional 747-400s and options on four more of the

Above: In 1988 Malaysian Airlines ordered two GE-powered 747-400 Combis, which were later followed by a number of purely passenger aircraft. MAS 747-4H6 9M-MHO (c/n 25126) was a passenger version delivered on 10 June 1991, but with the Asian economic difficulties it was sold to QANTAS as VH-OED in September 1998.
Malaysian Airlines System

PW4000-powered aircraft. By this time, five of the original order for 10 aircraft were in service. In November, Canadian Airlines confirmed its remaining options on four 747-400s, in addition to the three aircraft already ordered, the total value being $840 million. By the end of the year a total of 218 747-400s had been sold, of which 63 were ordered in 1989 — the majority in Asia — and a total of 44 had been delivered.

A rather disturbing incident occurred to a KLM 747-400 carrying 233 passengers from Amsterdam to Tokyo on 15 December 1989, when all four engines flamed out over Alaska. The Alaskan volcano, Mount Redoubt, had erupted a week previously resulting in a temporary closure of the airways until the ash had dispersed. In the belief that the danger had passed, the KLM airliner was the first to

Above: During the latter half of 1988 Air Canada ordered three 747-400 Combis. Air Canada 747-433 SCD Combi C-GAGN (c/n 25075) was delivered on 30 August 1991, and is seen in the airline's old livery on final approach to London Heathrow in June 1993. *Author*

Above: United has been a long-term operator of Boeing airliners powered by Pratt & Whitney engines. Boeing 747-422 N184UA (c/n 25380) was delivered to United on 1 May 1992. This aircraft is owned by Walt Disney and leased back to United, and is seen at Sydney in December 1992 in the airline's old livery. *Author*

Above: Air New Zealand initially ordered one 747-400 in 1988. Boeing 747-419 ZK-NBT (c/n 24855; l/n 815) was delivered on 31 October 1990. *Boeing*

Above: Canadian International ordered three CF6-powered 747-400s in the latter half of 1988. Canadian 747-475 C-GMWW (c/n 24883) was delivered on 11 December 1990, and is seen on final approach to Hong Kong Kai Tak in April 1998. *Author*

Above: Singapore Airlines took delivery of its first two 747-400s in March 1989. A later delivery was 9V-SMV (c/n 27069; l/n 1010), which was handed over on 22 December 1993, and is seen on approach to Hong Kong Kai Tak on 1 January 1995.
Asian Aviation Photography

Above: On 25 May 1989 the first 747-430, D-ABVA (c/n 23816), arrived at the Frankfurt base of Lufthansa, flying the flags of Germany and the USA. *Lufthansa*

penetrate the area, but what the crew did not know was that the volcano had erupted again an hour before the 747 entered the area at night. The crew was unaware the aircraft was penetrating the ash-cloud until the engines flamed out at 31,000ft. The crew managed to relight two of the engines at 13,000ft, the other two being started at 6,000ft, the aircraft landing safely at Anchorage. All four engines were changed and the aircraft was inspected for damage caused by abrasive dust, particularly to the windows.

In January 1990 Lufthansa announced its intention of ultimately increasing its 747-400 fleet to 56 aircraft, including the existing 15 on order and 15 options already held. Included in the total could be up to 15 -400Fs, but the additional aircraft could also consist of any of the -400 versions available; the value to Boeing could be in excess of $7.5 billion. Power for these aircraft was to come from the CF6-80C2 engine, with the possible purchase of some 200 engines worth well over $1 billion. In the same month SIA placed an order for a further 15 747-400s, with options on another 15 worth around $5.5 billion. Power would be from Pratt & Whitney PW4000s, and deliveries were scheduled to commence in 1994, once the 20 aircraft currently on order were in service. Also in January, Air France, which already had 12 747-400s on order, announced its takeover of UTA, which the previous September had taken

delivery of its own first two 747-400s, and these aircraft were absorbed into the Air France fleet.

By 1992 Japan Air System (JAS) planned to start a Narita to Honolulu service as its third international route, expanding to Bangkok, Hong Kong, Seoul and Singapore between 1993 and 1995. To achieve this expansion, it was reported in January 1990 that an order would be placed for eight 747-400s, with a leased aircraft following in 1995. JAS also had plans to operate to the US Midwest or East Coast, and to fly to various destinations in Europe. In February, QANTAS topped up its 747-400 fleet with another aircraft, and Cathay converted four options, taking its potential fleet to 24 aircraft. China Airlines (CAL) also took delivery in February of the first of five PW4000-powered 747-400s for services to the US West Coast, and Thai Airways accepted the first of three 747-400s for use on long-range services from Bangkok.

In March, El Al ordered two 747-400s with options on two more for delivery in 1993/4. The aircraft were to be configured with 12 First class, 46 Business class and 429 Tourist class seats. Two months later, JAL maintained its claim as the world's largest 747 operator with an order for 20 additional 747-400s and options on a further 34, making the 747 the first wide-bodied airliner to achieve more than 1,000 sales. This brought commitments by JAL for the 747-400 to 74, with five already in service and the balance due by 1999. Four of the 747-400s were to be the -400D domestic version, with reductions in weight, wingspan — for ease of ground-handling — and wing-bending moment, to reduce fatigue on the high-frequency domestic operations. Boeing was offering only 747-400 versions by this time, with just five -200Fs and a -300 Combi remaining to be delivered.

In a deal for 72 Boeing airliners worth a potential $4 billion, the People's Republic of China ordered five 747-400s in May for Air China, to be powered by P&W PW4056 engines. The following month Korean Air reserved a total of 23 747-400s. Along with additional Thai requirements, this took overall commitments to 307 aircraft; with only 71 delivered, there was now a substantial backlog.

In mid-1990 BA was in the process of finalising a $4.5 billion order with Boeing which would more than double the size of the airline's -400 fleet by the end of the decade. The order was reported to include firm commitments for 20 aircraft with 10 options, in addition to the 14 already in service and seven more to be delivered. The order was confirmed in July with a contract for 33 747-400s worth some $6.4 billion — somewhat larger than expected, and including 21 firm orders, seven of which were previous options taken up, with options on another 12. At the same time, Rolls-Royce gained an order for 160 engines worth £600 million.

Asiana was planning a massive fleet expansion, including an order for 48 Boeing airliners worth some $4.5 billion. Having started operations only in December 1988 in direct competition with Korean Air, Asiana commenced international services to Japan in January 1990 using 737-400s. Its existing orders included two 747-400s with two options, but the airline had a need for a further 20 747-400s, at least two of which were expected to be Freighters. The initial 747-400 Combis, configured for 230 passengers in two classes, also had room for 13 pallets on the main deck and were required for route expansion from Seoul to New York non-stop starting in 1991. By the end of 1992 Asiana expected to be operating to London, Paris and Frankfurt.

In June, Air India selected R-R RB211 engines for four 747-400s on order, with options on five more, but in October 1991 the Indian Government changed the engine selection to the PW4056. The first two on firm order were scheduled for delivery in 1992, with the second pair following in 1993. In July, KLM added two firm orders for 747-400Fs and options on two more, to add to its fleet of 10 Combis and five passenger versions. The 747-400Fs were to be powered by 55,000lb (243kN)-thrust CF6-80C2B1F engines. Even though some major airlines, including the American carriers, were experiencing falling load factors and increases in fuel prices due to the Gulf crisis in August 1990, Air France took out six more options on the 747-400, bringing its total orders to 20 firm plus 19 options, with deliveries to start in February 1991.

On 27 August 1990 United 747-400 N174UA suffered a serious emergency when it landed at Los Angeles International Airport after a flight from Sydney with the nose and fuselage main undercarriage units still retracted. The aircraft, which had been delivered in January, incurred only minor structural damage, as the Captain managed to hold the nose up for most of the 2.5km (1½-mile) landing roll. The 343 passengers and 20 crew evacuated via the emergency chutes and the runway was blocked for nearly eight hours while the aircraft was lifted with airbags, and the nose gear locked down.

In October, VARIG announced a $2.6 billion order for six CF6-80C2-powered 747-400s with options on five more. SIA increased its 1986 order for 747-400s, from 14 with six options to 15 plus 15, the additional firm order being for a Freighter. In November, Garuda ordered nine CF6-80C2-powered 747-400s, the original undisclosed order for six having been signed in 1989.

By the end of 1990, the 747-400 had become the most ordered version of the 747, with a total of 397 sold, taking Boeing's total sales for the year to double the previous record of 1988. Air India was able to convert five options to firm orders and had plans to add six further 747-400s in passenger configuration and three

Above: The redesigned galleys on the 747-400 make it easier for the cabin crew to service the refreshment needs of the passengers, particularly from the spacious rear galley. *Lufthansa*

Above: The First class seats on Lufthansa's 747-400s allow passengers room to relax or rest. *Lufthansa*

Above: In May 1989 South African Airways placed an order for two Rolls Royce-powered 747-400s for its services to Europe. *South African Airways*

Above: Along with JAL, ANA specified the Domestic version of the 747-400, without the distinctive winglets, for its high-density national routes. Boeing 747-481D JA8964 (c/n 27163; l/n 996) was delivered on 24 March 1994, and is seen at Osaka Airport in June 1994. *Asian Aviation Photography*

Above: UTA had taken delivery of the first of two 747-400s when it was taken over by Air France in January 1990. *Boeing*

to five cargo versions by the end of the century. Meanwhile, Cargolux had ordered three 747-400Fs with options on three more, with deliveries planned to start in 1994. The 100th 747-400 was delivered to Canadian Airlines in December, initially operating services to Hawaii.

By February 1991 the Gulf War was having a serious effect on airline operations, with not only the increased cost of fuel, but also a reluctance for people to risk flying, especially around the Gulf region. Even with the cessation of hostilities, the world's airlines saw only a slow recovery. However, JAL was prepared for the market recovery, expecting 15 new 747-400s to join the airline to bring its total fleet to 105 aircraft, of which 75 would be 747s, including 22 -400s. New airline orders announced in April included six 747-400s for SIA, one -400 with two options for Air New Zealand, four -400s for Air India, and six -400s plus six options for MAS.

The first of six 747-400Ds entered domestic service with JAL on 28 October 1991, with the second following on 1 November and the remaining four aircraft delivered the following year. Two corporate 747-400s were delivered to the Japanese Government by November to be used on VIP flights, but also to be available for international rescue operations, emergency aid transport and various other special missions.

In November 1991 Asiana took delivery of the first 747-400 Combi only three years after starting up in direct competition with Korean Air. At the time of the 747 delivery, Asiana was operating 300 domestic flights a week and more than 50 weekly international scheduled services within the Asia/Pacific region. The 747-400 fleet was ordered for operations across the Pacific to Los Angeles, the thrice-weekly service being inaugurated on 15 November. With the delivery of the second 747-400 in January, the services to Los Angeles became daily and a total of 20 747s was expected to be in service by the end of the decade. Six of this fleet had been specified as Freighters, with deliveries of these to begin one a year after the first two passenger versions had entered service in 1995. As the new passenger aircraft arrived, Asiana planned route expansion to other US destinations as well as Europe, starting with Paris.

Boeing ended 1991 having delivered a record number of airliners in one year, and having received a record number of orders including 38 747-400s, of which eight were ordered by BA and four more for QANTAS announced at the close of the year. This achievement was especially noteworthy, as, due to the Gulf crisis, its effect on world economics, a major reduction in air travel and over-ordering in 1989 and

Left: In March 1990 El Al ordered two 747-400s to allow expansion of its services to North America. El Al 747-458 4X-ELA (c/n 26055) was the first to be delivered, on 27 April 1994, and is seen on approach to London Heathrow in March 1999. *Author*

Left: With a new order for 20 747-400s placed in May 1990, JAL became potentially the largest 747 operator. JAL 747-446 JA8072 (c/n 24424; l/n 760) was delivered on 25 January 1990, and is seen in the airline's new colourscheme, departing Boeing Field. *Boeing*

Left: In mid-1990 BA ordered 34 more 747-400s, which would more than double the number in service with the airline. BA 747-436 G-BNLM (c/n 24055) was part of the original order and was delivered on 28 June 1990. It is seen on approach to London Heathrow in the new Denmark ('Wings') colours in March 1999. *Author*

1990, world jet airliner sales overall had dropped to 36% of the previous year's. The first of nine CF6-80C2-B1F-powered 747-400s entered service with VARIG at the turn of the year.

1992 opened with SIA converting four of its options to firm orders in a deal worth $600 million, and having 17 more options remaining, a number of which were expected to be Freighters. Major airlines were feeling the effects of the economic recession and in February United announced that deliveries of 122 Boeing airliners were being deferred. Its new delivery programme included six 747-400s in 1992, four in 1993, three in 1994 and three in 1995. After a year of unprecedented losses, United cut capital spending by $2 billion, although no aircraft orders were cancelled.

In February there were reports that the Sultan of Brunei wanted to acquire a 747-400 instead of the previously-ordered Airbus A340. Having close contacts with Lufthansa, which wished to defer an order for a 747-400 due in April, the Brunei Royal Flight made approaches to secure delivery, and the aircraft was refitted with a VIP interior.

In the first quarter of 1992, deliveries of Boeing airliners continued at record levels, with a total of 124 new aircraft completed including 16 747s, compared with the previous record total of 119 in the second quarter of 1991. Amongst deliveries was the first of five all-passenger 368-seat 747-400s for Air China, previous deliveries being of three -400 Combis. In April, Thai ordered another four 747-400s to add to the eight GE-powered aircraft already on order and the four which were in service, mainly

Above: Cathay Pacific made full use of the power from the RB211 turbofans for operation from the demanding Kai Tak Airport in Hong Kong. Cathay 747-467 B-HUJ (c/n 27595) was delivered on 23 May 1995, and is seen shortly after take-off from Kai Tak, with Central in the background. *Cathay Pacific*

Above: A number of airlines have used special colour schemes on their aircraft, to promote either their own operations or an ecological event, or simply to act as a flying billboard. SIA 747-412 9V-SPL (c/n 26557) was delivered on 30 January 1997; its fuselage has been painted in a special product-launch livery. *Singapore Airlines*

Above: Asiana commenced operations in December 1988, and in mid-1990 planned to order a further 20 747-400s, at least two of which would be Freighters. Asiana Cargo 747-48EF HL7422 (c/n 28367) was delivered on 18 December 1996, and is seen at Stansted in March 1999. *Nick Granger*

Above: At the end of 1990 Cargolux placed an initial order for three 747-400Fs. Cargolux 747-4R7F LX-LCV (c/n 29053) was part of a subsequent order, and was delivered on 19 December 1997. *Cargolux*

Above: In November 1990 Garuda Indonesia confirmed orders for nine 747-400s, but due to Asian economic difficulties only three were delivered, one of which had previously been allocated to VARIG. Garuda 747-4U3 PK-GSG (c/n 25704; l/n 1011) was the first to be delivered, on 14 January 1994. The 747-400s are used on long-haul flights to Europe. *Boeing*

on routes to Europe. Korean Air added seven -400s to its fleet, selecting the PW4056 engine in an order worth $270 million. However, half-year 747 orders were down, at 17 compared to 27 in the same period the previous year. In June, SIA confirmed two more options, taking total firm orders to 25.

Pilot training and currency has always been a problem with long-range jet airliners, SIA being typical, with pilots requiring at least three manual landings every three months, plus one Autoland every 45 days. With SIA's 300 747 pilots averaging 2.2 manual landings a month in 1992, the situation was expected to become worse as more crews joined the roster. The airline needed to schedule an average of 12 sectors a week for each of the 12 747-400s in service at the time just to maintain recency for the existing crews. As an example of the problem, the Singapore to London route alone occupied two aircraft, each with only seven sectors a week, giving an instant shortfall. With a planned fleet of 56 aircraft, each requiring 12½ two-man crews, even though some conversion work could be done on the simulator, crews would still have to acquire handling experience in the aircraft. SIA was periodically taking an aircraft out of service to allow conversion for groups of pilots in circuits around Changi Airport, but this was difficult to fit into operational schedules. SIA was therefore

considering dedicating one aircraft to crew training on a rotational basis to be available 24 hours a day for at least three weeks every month. A group of 22 pilots on training would occupy one aircraft for 16 days, flying three details a day, while 48 pilots would utilise the aircraft for 37 days. Although having one aircraft dedicated to training would be an expensive exercise, it would allow a more efficient use of pilot resources.

From August 1992, Boeing and Honeywell were working on defining a major update of the flight management computer (FMC) system in the 747-400, to incorporate the benefits of satellite-based navigation and communications to be introduced in 1994. In September 1992 QANTAS took delivery of its 100th Boeing airliner since operations were started — a 747-400 to be used on the Sydney to Los Angeles service. A further 747-400 was delivered the following month.

The cockpit canopy of the first 747-400F (Freighter) destined for Air France was completed in October 1992 for delivery in October 1993, following the flight development programme. Powered by CF6-80-C2 engines, the -400F had up to 18,200kg more payload than the -200F over ranges in excess of 8,300km (4,500nm).

Nine years after the shooting down of a Korean 747 in Russian airspace, Northwest

Above: Garuda's Executive class features two-abreast seating with leather upholstery.
Garuda Indonesian Airlines

pioneered new international airways across the same region on 12 October 1992. The 747-400 was flying the daily service from Detroit to Tokyo, and was the first US commercial aircraft to be flown on a scheduled service to Japan through Russian airspace, the final clearances being sanctioned just before departure from Detroit. As a result, travelling time and fuel-burn were reduced, allowing payloads to be increased marginally as fuel-loads were reduced. As an example, travel times from Detroit to Tokyo could be reduced by one hour on the westbound leg by passing well to the north of the seasonal winter headwinds. The airlines estimated that it would result in a collective saving of nearly $20 million annually. Operational advantages included reduced congestion on the north-Pacific airways.

In December ILFC confirmed an order for 81 airliners, with 25 options shared between Airbus and Boeing, the shopping list including three 747-400s. However, United was still experiencing financial difficulties, and was considering a number of outright cancellations. It had taken delivery of 18 of its total order for 45 747-400s, and it was believed that wide-body commitments were those most likely to be affected. Japan Airlines was also suffering from increasing losses, and was planning to defer at least 25 747-400s beyond 1998. These aircraft were part of a previously-unannounced commitment for 26 firm orders and 29 options held by JAL. The airline already had 25 in service and planned to take delivery of a further 15 by March 1998, a reduction of 11 aircraft. As a result of these and other announcements of deferred and cancelled orders being made almost weekly, Boeing was considering reducing the production rate of the 747-400 from five to three a month in the second quarter of 1994, although the order backlog still stood at 233 aircraft.

The board of the newly-privatised Philippine Airlines (PAL) had placed orders with Airbus and Boeing in August 1992, including one for four GE-powered Boeing 747-400s, which survived a boardroom battle and were confirmed in January 1993. However, the new board was replaced at the end of February, the orders being reviewed with the 747-400 order likely to be reduced to two aircraft. The following month PAL confirmed the order for two, with two options. In early 1993, BA set up a new subsidiary known as British Asia Airways (BAA) to start scheduled services between Taipei and London via Hong Kong twice a week. BAA wet-leased a 747-400 from BA, and the services started on 29 March.

At the end of February 1993 the first 747-400F was rolled off the Everett production

Above: Despite the economic effects of the Gulf crisis, in February 1991 JAL was preparing for the expected market recovery, with 15 more 747-400s to be delivered. These aircraft are used for long-haul flights to Europe and North America, and some regional services. JAL 747-446 JA8085 (c/n 25260; l/n 876) was delivered on 24 September 1991, and is seen on final approach to Hong Kong Kai Tak on a flight from Tokyo in November 1993. *Asian Aviation Photography*

Above: In October 1992 Northwest pioneered new international airways through Russian airspace, reducing the distance from North America to Tokyo. Northwest 747-451 N662US (c/n 23720; l/n 708) was delivered to Northwest on 16 March 1989, and is seen taxiing for departure at Hong Kong Kai Tak in November 1993. *Asian Aviation Photography*

Above: In 1993 BA set up a new subsidiary called British Asia Airways, to operate services from London to Taipei via Hong Kong using 747-400s leased from BA. BAA 747-436 G-CIVA (c/n 27092; l/n 967) was one of the aircraft allocated to this service, and is seen ready for departure from Kai Tak in April 1998. *Author*

Above: Boeing 747-436 G-CIVB (c/n 25811; l/n 1018) was delivered on 15 February 1994 and allocated to British Asia Airways; with the introduction of the new 'Citizen of the World' image it received the 'Chelsea Rose' tail design. It is used regularly on the London to Hong Kong route, and is seen on approach to London Heathrow in January 2000. *Nick Granger*

Above: Following the maiden flight of the 747-400 Freighter on 4 May 1993, orders for this variant included two for Cathay Pacific. Cathay 747-467F B-HUH (c/n 27175; l/n 1020) was delivered on 1 June 1994 as VR-HUH, and is seen ready for departure from Hong Kong Kai Tak in April 1998. *Author*

line to complete a cargo-loading demonstration before being prepared for the flight development programme. Provision was made for additional cargo space on the upper deck, and with changes on the main deck and the underfloor cargo hold, a further 41.7cu m of space was available compared with the 747-200F. The first 747-400F made its maiden flight on 4 May 1993, starting a three-month flight test programme, by which time 16 orders had been received, from Air France with four, Asiana three, Cargolux three, Cathay Pacific two, KLM two and SIA two, with the first delivery due in October. Air France, however, needed to defer or cancel a total of 23 aircraft between 1993 and 1996, including the 747-400Fs, discussions taking place in August to resolve the issues, which included European certification.

Like JAL, JAS was also experiencing financial difficulties by March 1993 and, as part of a $869 million cost-cutting exercise, took six Boeing 777s instead of six 747-400s, and delayed deliveries in an effort to buy extra time to recover financially. Thai Airways also requested deferred delivery of one 747-400 by 12-15 months, amongst other deferrals and cancellations of options. In contrast to the cut-backs in orders, Air

India was looking forward to its first substantial fleet additions for more than a decade with the delivery of four 747-400s between August 1993 and March 1994, replacing some of the earlier 747-200s. The airline was amongst the 10 most profitable in the world, achieved with improved yields and some cost-cutting measures. The total cost of the new 747-400s was $682 million, and the 417-seat aircraft were initially deployed on the Mumbai (Bombay)-London-New York service, allowing the airline to expand its network.

A major milestone was reached on 10 September 1993, when the 1,000th 747 was rolled off the Everett production line. This was the fourth jet airliner to achieve 1,000 aircraft, following the 707, 727 and 737, and this particular 747-400 was handed over to SIA on 14 October.

On 12 September an Air France 747-400 overran the airfield at Tahiti after landing well down the runway. The aircraft left the runway to the right and came to a halt nose-down in shallow water with minor damage. Engines 2, 3 and 4 had reverse thrust deployed, but No 1 did not, and was still running after the incident. No fault was found with the GE CF6-80C2 FADEC system.

Above: The 1,000th 747 was rolled off the Everett production line on 10 September 1993; 747-412 9V-SMU (c/n 27063) was handed over to SIA on 13 October. *Singapore Airlines*

At the end of September, Air France announced the cancellation or delay to deliveries of 23 airliners, including the deferral of the first of four 747-400Fs due to be accepted in November.

With FAA certification achieved for the 747-400F and European approval awarded in November 1993, Cargolux won US permission to operate round-trip scheduled cargo flights to Los Angeles, starting in November when the first Freighter was delivered. The second aircraft was delivered in December, replacing a 747-200F on routes to the US West Coast, and giving a 14.2% reduction in fuel-burn and an increase in payload of about 20 tonnes, to 110 tonnes. During development-testing, the

Above: In February 1994 SIA took advantage of the soft market conditions to request bids from Airbus and Boeing to obtain the keenest prices between the 747-400 and A340-300. SIA already had 23 747-400s in service, with a further 13 on firm order. SIA 747-412 9V-SPH (c/n 26555) was delivered on 7 March 1996, and is seen ready to turn on to the runway at London Heathrow in April 1997. *Author*

Above: Although the depressed world economy was slowing down air travel, Air India was looking forward to a fleet expansion, with the first of four 747-400s entering service in August 1993 on services to New York. Air India 747-437 SCD VT-ESM (c/n 27078) was delivered on 4 August 1993, and is seen at London Heathrow a year later. *Author*

Above: Air India is one of many airlines now offering real-time communications for business or pleasure, with skyphones available on its 747-400s. *Air India*

Above: In January 1996, MAS confirmed an order for 10 747-400s, to add to its 10 passenger and two Combi versions already in service. Malaysian 747-4H6 9M-MPC (c/n 25700) was delivered on 10 May 1993, and is seen on final approach to Hong Kong Kai Tak in April 1998. *Author*

Above: The First class cabin in the MAS 747-400 is served by cabin crew in typical formal national dress. *Malaysian Airlines System*

Above: With FAA certification awarded, Cargolux took delivery of the first 747-400F in November 1993, starting services to Los Angeles. Cargolux 747-4R7F LX-KCV (c/n 25868) was delivered on 26 August 1997, and is seen loading through the upward-opening nose door. *Cargolux*

Cargolux 747-400F was found to have a 2,000kg lighter empty weight, allowing the maximum freight payload to increase to around 113,000kg over ranges of up to 8,100km (4,400nm). The greater range and payload was to be used to develop new markets, not only to the US West Coast but also over other long-distance routes. The improvement in productivity and efficiency achieved with its first two -400Fs made a substantial contribution to Cargolux's return to profit, enabling a further aircraft to be ordered in

Above: In addition to the nose door, the Cargolux 747-400F freighters feature an upward-opening door on the port side of the fuselage, to allow the carriage of taller cargo items in the middle and rear cabin. *Cargolux*

Above: El Al took delivery of its first two 747-400s in April and May 1994. Boeing 747-458 4X-ELD (c/n 29328) was delivered on 24 May 1999, and was the first to be painted in the airline's new livery. *El Al Israeli Airlines*

mid-1995 for delivery in the last quarter of the year, with a fourth delivered in August 1997.

Another runway overrun incident occurred with CAL 747-400 B-165 on 4 November 1993 at Hong Kong Kai Tak Airport, and although the aircraft was a write-off, all 296 people on board survived. The aircraft landed on Runway 13 in squally weather with high turbulence caused by

a nearby tropical storm. Surface winds were reported as 060 degrees at 20kt, gusting to 30kt, with a windshear warning and heavy rain.

In November BA announced the cancellation of seven options for 747-400s, reducing its commitment to 51 aircraft. Soon after, Boeing confirmed a production drop from five aircraft a month to three from February 1994, and down

Above: The El Al Economy/Tourist class features seat-back video screens as part of the passenger entertainment system. *El Al Israeli Airlines.*

Above: In mid-1996 United ordered up to 37 747-400s, including options and commitments for a possible stretched, high-capacity version. United 747-422 N193UA (c/n 26890) was delivered on 7 August 1996, and is seen at Washington Dulles in May 1999. *Author*

Above: Amongst the orders received at the end of 1996 was one for a 747-400 from Virgin Atlantic. Boeing 747-4Q8 G-VFAB (c/n 24958; l/n 1028) was originally allocated to JAS, but was delivered to Virgin on 28 April 1994; it is seen at London Heathrow about to turn on to the runway in April 1997. *Author*

Above: VARIG operated three 747-400s between 1991 and 1994 on lease from ILFC. The first example, 747-441 PP-VPG (c/n 24956; l/n 917), was delivered on 1 June 1992, and is seen on arrival at Hong Kong Kai Tak from Rio de Janeiro in August 1993. It was returned to ILFC in September 1994, and later entered service with Garuda. *Asian Aviation Photography*

Above: EVA Air was launched in mid-1991, and by mid-1997 had 10 747-400 Combis and two pure passenger versions, the Combis generating high revenue with premium cargo as well as passengers. Boeing 747-45E B16401 (c/n 27062; l/n 942) was the first delivered on 2 November 1992. *EVA Air/Ellis Communications*

Left: At the beginning of 1995 Air France was still experiencing economic difficulties and was considering cancelling all outstanding orders, including four 747-400s. Air France 747-4B3 Combi F-GEXB (c/n 24155) was originally delivered on 26 July 1991 to UTA, which merged with Air France in December 1992; it is seen on final approach to Hong Kong Kai Tak in April 1998. *Author*

Left: PAL experienced both financial difficulties and turbulent management in the early part of 1995, reducing its ability to finance its planned fleet of 747-400s. PAL 747-4F6 N753PR (c/n 27828; l/n 1039), originally allocated to JAL but delivered to PAL on 27 April 1995 on lease from Pearl Aircraft Ltd, is seen ready for departure from Hong Kong Kai Tak in April 1998. *Author*

Above: Following the end of the Gulf War, Kuwait Airways had to rebuild its fleet, placing orders for three 747-400s, although only one was delivered. This was 747-469 Combi 9K-ADE (c/n 27338; l/n 1046), which was delivered on 29 November 1994, and is seen on approach to London Gatwick in May 1995. This aircraft has since been sold. *Nick Granger*

Above: As well as ordering five 747-400s for itself, CAL also ordered one PW4056-powered 747-400 for its wholly-owned subsidiary Mandarin Airlines, which was intended for use on the route from Taipei to Vancouver. However, in practice, the aircraft is used more on Asian regional services. Boeing 747-409 B16801 (c/n 27965; l/n 1063) was delivered on 14 June 1995, and is seen at Hong Kong Kai Tak on turnaround. *Asian Aviation Photography*

to just two a month in January 1995. With the end of the year approaching, ILFC placed orders for seven more Boeing airliners including one 747-400. However, Boeing experienced a net reduction of 25 orders for the 747-400 during 1993.

In January 1994 United agreed to take delivery of two 747-400s which had been originally built for Northwest, but cancelled in August 1993; the main change was to reconfigure the aircraft with PW4056 engines. On 18 February 1994 SIA requested new bids from Airbus and Boeing to convert outstanding options to firm orders, which included 11 747-400s, with a further 11 options. SIA was believed to be taking advantage of the soft market conditions to drive the prices down; it already had 23 P&W-powered 747-400s in operation, with firm orders for another 13. In addition SIA had five 747-400Fs on order with 13 options. SIA was expected to choose between the 747-400 and the A340-300, and all three major engine manufacturers had been asked to bid. Meanwhile El Al, with the first of its two 747-400s due for delivery, was negotiating

for a third in March 1994 with the possibility of a fourth in 1995.

After a rather quiet 1994, there were signs of an improving economy as the year came to an end, with CAL announcing plans to order 46 new passenger aircraft over the next decade, and an intention to replace its older 747-200s with 747-400s around the year 2000. It already operated five 747-400s, and a further aircraft was ordered for its wholly-owned subsidiary Mandarin Airlines, this being delivered in June 1995 for services on the Taipei to Vancouver route.

At the start of 1995 Air France still had financial problems, and threatened to cancel all outstanding orders, including that for four 747-400s. However, a compromise deal reached in mid-1995 saw the reinstatement of the order for a 747-400F, as well as for other aircraft. On a more positive note, United, with 24 747-400s already in service, ordered two 747-400s in April for delivery by June 1996.

In June the long-awaited order was announced from Saudi Arabian Airlines for up to 60 airliners shared between Boeing and

Above: Due to the Asian economic difficulties, Korean Air was amongst the airlines facing cutbacks due to mounting losses. By mid-1998 KAL was in discussion with Boeing over deferring three 747-400s; in addition to other deferrals this caused Boeing to plan a reduction in 747-400 production, to one aircraft per month, by 2000. KAL 747-4B5 HL7484 (c/n 26392; l/n 893) was delivered on 28 January 1992, and is seen at Zurich in March 1992. *Nick Granger*

Above: Following protracted negotiations, the financially-ailing Canadian Airlines International was taken over by Air Canada in 1999. A number of CAI aircraft had adopted a new 'Snow Goose' livery towards the end of the year. Boeing 747-475 C-GMWW '881' (c/n 24883; l/n 823) was delivered on 11 December 1990, and is seen ready for departure from Toronto. The Canadian identity is being retained, at least for the time being, but the Air Canada logo now dominates the fin, with the Snow Goose appearing smaller on the fuselage. *Gary Tahir*

McDonnell Douglas. Included in this order were five 747-400s, but Saudi Arabia was having difficulty financing the new aircraft. The order was confirmed on 26 October 1995, the five 747-400s being powered by CF6-80C2s, and deliveries were planned to start in 1997, although there were still questions over the details of the funding for the $6 billion deal for 61 aircraft.

PAL was continuing to experience turbulent management, with conflict between the private owners controlling 67% of the airline and the Philippine Government, which held the remaining share. In March 1995 PAL announced an initiative to spend $125 million on a restructuring and expansion, to reverse the financial decline by making it more efficient and competitive. Included in the expansion was a plan to order two more 747-400s; however, with the airline already close to its debt:equity ratio, the plan to purchase a fourth 747-400 had to be abandoned. Garuda, after taking delivery of two GE-powered 747-400s and leasing a third from ILFC, was having difficulty raising the finance to

purchase the other six aircraft on order, and started negotiations with Boeing to achieve better terms. Agreement was reached in mid-1996, with one 747-400 order replaced by five 737-500s, and the other five deferred until at least 2000. In July KLM ordered two more 747-400 Combis powered by CF6-80 turbofans, bringing its total commitment to 13 aircraft.

The first half of 1995 showed some improvement in the orders for jet airliners, with an industry-wide order intake of 250 aircraft. The Boeing share was 149 new orders, with a net increase of 10 747-400s, bringing its total production backlog to 105 aircraft. A further boost was obtained in September when MAS announced plans to order 25 new widebody airliners, which was believed to include up to 10 more 747-400s and a similar number of options. MAS already had 10 747-400s and two Combis in operation, with another delivery due in 1996. The MAS order was confirmed on 9 January 1996 for 10 P&W PW4056-powered 747-400s and three options, with deliveries starting in early 1997.

Above: Air France has been a long-term operator of the 747 variants. Boeing 747-428 F-GITF (c/n 25602) was delivered on 7 April 1992. *C. Gambon/Air France*

Above: In June 1995 Saudi Arabian Airlines ordered 60 airliners from Boeing and McDonnell Douglas, including five 747-400s. *Saudi Arabian Airlines*

Above: The first 747-400s for Saudi Arabian Airlines were handed over on 22 December 1997, and a unique feature of these aircraft was a special prayer area for Muslim passengers, located behind the 10-abreast Guest (Economy) class with an individual passenger entertainment system screen in each seat-back. *Saudi Arabian Airlines*

Also in September, Lufthansa announced orders for 18 aircraft, with four 747-400s for delivery in 1997. There were also hopes in October that China would be placing orders for up to five more 747-400s with the first entering service in August 1996.

Following the liberation of Kuwait on 26 February 1991, Kuwait Airways was faced with a major rebuild of the fleet after 15 airliners had been stolen by the Iraqis (although eight were eventually recovered) and the airline's premises destroyed. By October 1995, 19 new aircraft had been delivered including three 747-400s, the first arriving in April of that year, but the other two aircraft were not delivered, and the first one was sold.

China Southern Airlines decided in October 1995 to lease two 747-400s for two years from March 1996 as an interim measure while the deliveries of six 777-200s were awaited. With the improvement in airliner sales during 1995, Boeing decided to raise production rates towards the end of 1996, taking 747 production from two to an average of 3.5 per month.

United Airlines was in final negotiations with Boeing for up to 35 aircraft in May 1996, which was expected to include up to 13 747-400s, the airline already having 24 in service. In July the order was revised by selecting fewer than the expected number of 777s, and increasing the 747-400 commitment to 37 aircraft. Firm orders were for 19 747s with options on 11, with positions reserved on seven which could be delivered after 2000 as a stretched version. In May BA was also reported to be close to finalising a $2 billion order for 20 Boeing airliners, including up to 15 747-400s, in addition to the current backlog covering 17 aircraft and options on nine. In mid-1996, Asiana signed Memoranda of Understanding (MoUs) for three additional 747-400 Combis plus three options to add to its fleet of 19 CF6-80C2-powered 747-400s.

During 1996, jet airliner orders exceeded 1,000, and production rates were set to rise to record levels over the following two to three years. Boeing made 75 747-400 sales during the year, but had nine cancellations. There were 26 747s delivered, leaving a backlog of 161. End-of-year orders for one 747-400 from Virgin, two Combis from Air China and a further -400F from Cargolux contributed to the total.

In mid-1997 BA introduced its controversial new image, with 50 artists commissioned globally to provide 'Citizen of the World' designs on the aircraft fins, leaving only Concorde with a stylised Union Flag. After a major portion of the fleet had been repainted, the decision was taken in mid-1999 to standardise on the stylised Union Flag across the entire fleet.

In June, Atlas Air confirmed plans to buy ten CF6-80C2-powered 747-400Fs with options on a further ten, the total value being around $1.7 billion. The first four aircraft in the firm order were scheduled for delivery in 1998, with the remainder due in 1999 and 2000. In August,

Asiana gained Korean Government approval for orders with Airbus and Boeing, including a 747-400F, in the first phase of an expansion programme. The second phase was expected to include two 747-400s, a major condition being a 20% industrial offset.

With the increase in production rates caused by the new order backlog across the range of airliners, Boeing was experiencing difficulties with meeting the delivery schedules of 747-400s, and moved several hundred assembly workers from the adjacent 767 line to help avoid delays. Some of the delays were caused by late arrival of subassemblies, parts and equipment, but, having let many experienced workers go in the past, Boeing was also having to cope with the steep learning-curve of the newly-recruited labour. One of the 747-400s due for delivery in 1997 was expected to slip into 1998, but Boeing was working to achieve all 58 747 deliveries scheduled for 1998. The situation had become worse by October, when Boeing had temporarily to halt production of 747s and Next Generation 737s to allow suppliers time to make up the parts shortages which had delayed deliveries and caused costly out-of-sequence assembly. Production of the 747 was halted for 20 days, and Boeing expected at this stage to deliver four or five fewer than planned by the end of the year. However, the shutdown of the 747 line continued into mid-November, with delays to ANA, Asiana and Saudi orders, and was now likely to result in deliveries of at least 21 aircraft being delayed until 1998. It was estimated that the cost of the recovery plans and late-delivery payments for both the 737 and 747 were in the region of $2.6 billion.

EVA Airways of Taiwan had been launched in mid-1991, and by 1997 had a fleet of 30 new jet airliners serving a network to London, New York and Panama City, and had been earning healthy annual profits since 1995. Included in the long-haul fleet were 12 747-400s, of which 10 were Combis, and an additional passenger 747-400 was delivered by the end of the year, with two more to follow by April 1998. The Combis were flying on daily schedules to the USA, often with premium freight, resulting in cargo generating around one third of the airline's revenue.

With the success of the 747-400Fs in operation with Cargolux, the Luxembourg-based all-cargo airline placed orders for a further five Freighters in September, with options on two more, to replace the three remaining 747-200Fs and add to the existing fleet of four -400Fs. The first two aircraft were scheduled for delivery by the end of 1998, with the fleet growing to 10 by mid-1999. Despite the fact that its existing -400Fs were GE CF6-80C2B1F-powered, Cargolux specified Rolls-Royce RB211-524HT hybrid engines for the new aircraft.

The long-awaited order from China for new Boeing airliners was finally approved in Washington DC on 30 October 1997, and covered 50 aircraft worth $3 billion. Included in the order was one 747-400 for Air China, although this aircraft appeared to be part of a previous purchase covering five 747s, of which two were Combis.

The financial aspects of the Saudi Arabian Airlines order for 61 aircraft had still not been settled by August 1997 when the first aircraft was ready for delivery. By November the first 747 was being delayed due to the lack of finance and the airline was negotiating a $4.33 billion Government-guaranteed loan to overcome the problems. Finance was finally approved in time for the handover of the first four aircraft to Saudi Arabian on 22 December, these being one 747-400 and one 777-200, plus an MD-11F and an MD-90. In December, Lufthansa announced a further expansion of its long-haul fleet to include five 747-400s together with unspecified options, with the definite orders to be fulfilled between 2000 and 2002.

By the end of 1997 the jet airliner order boom appeared to have slowed down, no doubt influenced by the growing economic crisis in Asia, which had been the main source of orders for large wide-bodied airliners. During the year Boeing sold 37 747s with no cancellations, and with 39 deliveries had an order backlog of 159 aircraft. However, a number of the Asian carriers were considering deferring orders, or, in the case of PAL, outright cancellations. Boeing was exposed in the longer term, with 48 747s as well as 93 777s for the Asian market accounting

Below: On 21 October 1999 Air Namibia took delivery of 747-48E Combi V5-NMA (c/n 28551; l/n 1131), originally allocated to Asiana. It is seen on finals to London Heathrow in January 2000. *Nick Granger*

for about a third of the total backlog of deliveries. By March 1998 even the Asian market-leader, SIA, announced the delay in delivery of one 747 by 13 months until March 2000, and PAL was deferring two more 747s, making a total of six, with two aircraft still planned for delivery in the second half of 1998. PAL was forced to abandon all international flights due to financial problems in October 1998, but, with the four 747-400s released by a US court decision, international flights were relaunched on 29 October. QANTAS was also considering acquiring up to six surplus 747-400s from Asian operators, to be used on the new three-times-a-week services, from Sydney to Buenos Aires via Auckland, from Sydney to Zurich via Singapore, and from Melbourne to London via Hong Kong. MAS announced a large loss for the year ending 31 March 1998, and rescheduled deliveries of three 747s due in both 1999 and 2000 — two for March/April 2001, two for February/March 2002 and the final pair for October 2003. The remaining four 747s of the original order were already in service, but two were on offer to QANTAS, and a buyer was being sought for the two -400 Combis. By mid-year, KAL was in negotiation with Boeing to defer three 747-400s and one -400F due for delivery in 1999. As a result of these and other cutbacks, Boeing announced a reduction in the monthly 747 production rate from five to 3.5 in the second quarter of 1999, and to one a month in 2000. Ironically, the massive production problems had been overcome just in time for the market to make one of its periodic downturns; if production of the 747 — Boeing's biggest money-maker – reduced to one per month, the cut in revenue would make the finance of future developments more difficult. At the end of 1998, deliveries of 747s totalled 49 for the year, with 48 more due in the next year. Without significant new orders, only 12 would be scheduled for completion in 2000, the previous 'low' having been in 1984, with 15 deliveries.

Despite the continuing Asian economic difficulties, JAL took delivery of its 100th 747 in November 1998, confirming the airline as the biggest operator of the type. JAL had 82 747s in service, including 35 -400s used on international and domestic routes; outstanding orders included 15 more 747-400s. Following orders for up to seven 777s placed in November 1995, SAA and Boeing were unable to agree on industrial offsets and at the end of 1998 two 'white-tail' (unused) 747-400s built for PAL were exchanged for the 777 order and delivered to SAA in December. Together with two other recent deliveries, these brought the SAA -400 fleet to eight aircraft. The RB211-powered 747-400s were initially operated on increased frequencies to London.

In February 1999, City Bird, the low-cost, long-haul Belgian carrier, ordered two new 747-400Fs for delivery in June and July 2000 worth $340 million. The aircraft were planned for long-haul services to South America and East and West Coast destinations in the USA. KLM was reported to be considering an order for four more 747-400s in February, to add to the 19 already in service, 14 of which were Combis. In March, MAS announced the sale of some aircraft as part of a rationalisation programme. Two GE-powered 747-400 Combis were to be sold as new P&W-powered 747-400s on order entered service; at this point MAS had 15 747-400s in operation, with six still to be delivered.

In April, as part of a significant expansion of its cargo operations, EVA Airways ordered three CF6-80C2-powered 747-400Fs, the first due for delivery in 2000, these aircraft being ideal for the long-haul routes from southeast Asia to Europe and the USA. In 1998 cargo generated 41% of EVA's total revenue, and this was expected to reach 50% within three years. The following month CAL announced an order for 12 747-400Fs, subject to Taiwanese Government approval, as part of a fleet rationalisation. By the time official approval was obtained in August, the order for 747s had increased to 13 747-400Fs with four options and two passenger 747-400s. Although P&W had been a long-term engine supplier to CAL, GE offered a better deal and its CF6-80C2 turbofans were selected for the 747s.

In May, Atlas Air took delivery of its fifth 747-400F and wet-leased the aircraft to BA World Cargo painted in the latter's colours — the first all-cargo 747 in BA livery since its

Above: Korean Air placed early orders for three 747-400s, with options on a further three to connect Korea with destinations in Europe and North America. KAL 747-4B5 HL7477 (c/n 24198; l/n 729) was the first delivery, on 13 June 1989. *Boeing*

747-200F was sold to Cathay in 1982. The new aircraft replaced an Atlas-liveried 747-400F which had been operating with BA since August 1998.

In October, Cathay announced an order for two 747-400Fs powered by RB211-524 engines for delivery in September 2000 and August 2001. Also in October 1999, Air Namibia took delivery of a 747-400 Combi originally ordered (but cancelled) by Asiana. The CF6-80C2-powered aircraft replaced a 747SP leased from SAA, and provided the extra cargo capacity needed to serve the transport requirements of the Namibian fishing industry.

Boeing introduced new assembly processes for the 747 in September 1999, using a computer-defined snap-together technique developed on the 777 and updated 767. The aim was to reduce flow-time by 40% over the next five years, allowing an aircraft to be produced in an average cycle time of six months. The improvement programme had been underway for some five years, costing $400 million as an investment in the future of the 747.

The process had begun with digitising the original 1960s drawings to create a database that used the CATIA (computer-aided three-dimensional application) design and manufacturing system. Northrop Grumman, which builds the major parts of the 747 fuselage, used the new database to produce more accurate panels. The new technique combined the accurate fuselage assembly (AFA) process, jointly defined by Northrop Grumman and Boeing in 1994, with the work done by the fuselage assembly improvement team (FAIT) in modifying Boeing's tooling and manufacture at Everett. The AFA simplifies assembly techniques whereby precision holes in the more accurate panels and other parts of the structure enable parts to self-locate. The precision fit is achieved by using laser-alignment and computer-controlled positioning systems, making redundant the traditional assembly jigs and tools which were expensive to maintain and to keep within tolerances. Not only has the need for expensive reworking been reduced by a factor of 4:1, but quality of assembly is also improved. Should the go-ahead be given for a stretched 747 development with a wing-root extension, then Boeing expects to follow with the digitising of the wing. The first aircraft to benefit from the full package of new fuselage assembly processes was line-number 1236, a 747-400 for JAL delivered in November 1999.

Above: On 26 January 1989 the first of 14 747-400s was delivered to Northwest — the initial airline to put this new version into service, starting with domestic operations. When sufficient experience had been built up, the 747-400s were allocated to trans-Pacific routes to Asia. Boeing 747-451 N668US (c/n 24223; l/n 800) was delivered on 26 July 1990, and is seen departing from Hong Kong Kai Tak on 26 June 1990. *Asian Aviation Photography*

Above: Cathay Pacific was the first airline to take delivery of an RB211-powered 747-400, which was handed over on 8 June 1989. Cathay 747-467 B-HOY (c/n 25351) was delivered on 22 November 1991, and is seen on approach to Hong Kong Kai Tak in April 1998. *Author*

Above: KAL also requested the deferral of one 747-400F. Earlier Boeing 747-4B5F HL7497 (c/n 26401; l/n 1087) was delivered on 6 September 1996, and is seen with both nose and rear-fuselage upward-opening cargo-doors open. *Korean Air Lines*

Above: During 1999 Virgin Atlantic adopted a new colourscheme with the Union Jack featured on the winglets. Boeing 747-4Q8 G-VFAB (c/n 24958; l/n 1028) was delivered on lease from ILFC on 28 April 1994, and was the first aircraft to feature the new livery. It is seen on approach to London Heathrow in January 2000. *Author*

5. FUTURE DEVELOPMENTS

Above: In September 1989 Air France placed the launch order for the 747-400F nose-loading cargo version. *Boeing*

While the airliner manufacturer is attempting to obtain a return on the vast investment of producing a new airliner, or making major modifications to an existing model to maintain a long production run, airlines are constantly demanding more range and payload with improved economy to maintain their own competitive edge.

Once the Boeing 747-400 was established in service in response to market demands in the early 1990s, the three major Western airliner manufacturers were studying designs for aircraft with at least half as many seats again as the 747-400, and in two cases even considering up to 1,000-seaters. This requirement was driven by the growing congestion at major airports, with their inability to handle significant increases in aircraft movements. The only way major hub airports would be able to cope with the increased demand for air travel was for airlines to use larger aircraft on the high-density long-range routes. Amongst the challenges would be to make these larger aircraft capable of using the current facilities without too much modification, the tendency being towards an extended-upper-deck fuselage. Some airports were already stretched to the limit by the dimensions and passenger capacity of the Boeing 747-400.

Although the proposed Future Large Aircraft (FLA) being proposed by Boeing as part of the 747-X programme consisted of a 747-400 stretch and a 747-400 double-deck, a new double-deck design was also being considered. The larger airliner project, which would be completely new, would use much of the 747-400 experience. It would not be a replacement, but would be complementary, since the 747-400 would still fly routes requiring lower capacity over long ranges. The 747-X started as a market study with at least 40% more seats, the largest capacity being for many as 750 passengers.

A simple stretch of the 747-400 was the option which appealed most to the airlines, including QANTAS, which saw it as being the lowest-cost and quickest to produce, with a fit into existing airports. The stretch was expected to have two 3.55m plugs in the fuselage, one forward and the other aft of the wing, making a total length of 77.6m, increasing a typical three-class layout from 400 to 484 passengers. Because of the additional 14,060kg structural weight caused by strengthening the undercarriage, wing box and auxiliary wing spar, the stronger wing of the 747-400F Freighter would be used, and range would be reduced by 20%.

Above: In January 1990 SIA announced a further order for 15 747-400s. SIA 747-412 9V-SPE (c/n 26554) was delivered on 13 October 1995, and is seen taxiing to the holding point at Hong Kong Kai Tak in April 1998. *Author*

The double-deck adaptation of the basic 747-400 increased the three-class capacity to 560 passengers, with empty weight increased by about 17,230kg and a range reduced by 27% of the 747-400's, to around 13,400km.

An all-new widebody design was expected to seat up to 612 passengers in a double-deck layout, comprising 36 First class, 114 Business and 198 Economy on the main deck, with 264 Economy on the upper deck. With a stretch, later versions would be able to carry up to 750 passengers up to 14 seats abreast. This would have a larger wing and tail and a circular widebody fuselage, and be powered by four high-bypass engines on short wing pylons. The aircraft was to have had a similar wheelbase and length to the 747-400, making it more compatible with existing airports, and the initial version would have had a similar range to the 747-400 and a gross weight of around 545,000kg.

The major market for these larger airliners was seen to be Asia for the pan-Pacific routes. By mid-1992 Boeing was planning on bringing together later in the year up to eight major airlines in an advisory group to discuss plans for the FLA and to attempt to determine a common requirement. The plan was to narrow down the range of options to two or three of the most acceptable layouts from around a dozen basic configurations so far considered. With the limitations of a 747-400 development, some of the airlines were keener on the all-new aircraft to achieve the required pan-Pacific range of 8,000 nautical miles (15,000km), while Japan was more interested in a new, high-capacity version of the 747-400SR with 550 seats, but required only on short-range routes. Because of these conflicting requirements, Boeing could see the line of development being in two stages: a stretched 747-400 (747-500) initially and, later, the all-new design (787).

The all-new aircraft would be a double-deck design with the same length as the 747-400 at 67m, and a wingspan of over 80m with outer wing folding, similar to the never-used option for the 777, to be compatible with existing airport gates; the wing fold would bring a weight and drag penalty. A possible configuration for the fuselage was to have a new main circular cross-section for 12-abreast seating in Economy, with a smaller circular cross-section built on to the top capable of taking Economy seats up to nine abreast.

Performance enhancements were expected to give an improvement of around 9% in cruise efficiency, with 6% coming from advanced wing design, and hybrid laminar-flow techniques being considered for drag-reduction to achieve a cruise speed of Mach 0.865. The remaining improvements were expected to come from the engines, with the airlines suggesting using the existing large turbofans already being offered for the 777 and Airbus A330. With the existing 747-400 costing in the region of $160 million, the airlines were keen to cap the costs of the new aircraft at $250 million. The thrust requirements for a 650-seat 15,000km-range 747-X would be between 80,000lb and 85,000lb (356kN and 380kN) which was similar to the power for the 777, giving a climb-thrust requirement 4-8% greater than that for the 777. The thrust requirements for the 800-seater would be in the region of 100,000lb per engine. Even with a 24-wheel main undercarriage layout, the pavement loading would be marginally higher than with current types, requiring about 12% of the world's usable runways to be strengthened. Because of the increased size, it was believed that external video cameras would be required for the crew to judge the position of the undercarriage in relation to the edges of taxiways, aprons and runways.

As outlined in Chapter 4, sales of jet airliners decreased significantly during 1992, with the resulting cut-backs in production planned in 1993. However, Boeing had prior experience of developing a new airliner in times of economic recession, and managing to have the new aircraft ready for service as the market cycle began its upturn.

In April 1993 Boeing announced plans for performance improvements of the 747-400 to be introduced in two phases, the initial modifications being available by the end of the year and the more significant engineering changes becoming available by mid-1996. The phase 1 performance improvement package (PIP) included a redesigned, longer-chord dorsal fin fairing to give improved drag characteristics, made from composite material instead of aluminium. The fuel-transfer system from the tailplane tanks was to be slowed as the centre tanks emptied, to keep the fuel aft of the centre of gravity for as long as possible to improve trim-drag and reduce fuel-burn. The wing spoilers were rigged-down to a higher load to prevent float-up under negative pressure during the cruise, causing additional drag. The gross weight of the aircraft was increased by an initial 2,000lb (900kg) — equivalent to 10 passengers — with further increases planned. The PIP was expected to result in maximum gross take-off weight (MGTOW) increasing from 395,400kg to 422,700kg, with a typical range increase from 13,300km to 14,800km (8,000nm). The phase 1 changes were flight-tested on a leased United Airlines 747-400 later in April, with all new aircraft being fitted with the PIP by the end of the year, and all features available for retrofit to earlier aircraft.

The phase 2 improvements were to give further range enhancements, but required significant structural strengthening, with a decision on whether to proceed needed by the end of the year. The increase in gross weight had to be determined, and locations had to be found for additional fuel, the remaining space in the tailplane being capable of holding between 1,800 and 2,400gal US (6,800 to 9,000 litres). To cope with the extra weight, a heavier-gauge wing skin would be required, particularly on the top and bottom inboard wing, as would a strengthened centre section and undercarriage. These phase 2 improvements were expected to be incorporated in the planned 747-X, with a 6m increase in fuselage length and the same MGTOW as the improved 747-400.

By the time of the Paris Show in June 1993, Boeing was working with potential launch customers to narrow down the five concepts for the 747-X/NLA (New Large Aircraft) to two versions by the end of July, with a final baseline design targeted for the end of the year. The nine airlines in the consultative group consisted of five carriers from the Asia/Pacific region — All Nippon Airways, Japan Airlines, Cathay Pacific, Singapore Airlines and QANTAS — plus Air France, British Airways and Lufthansa in Europe, and United as the sole representative from the USA. To meet the expected requirement for a long-range, high-capacity airliner available around the end of the century, the five new concepts included four all-new designs and the re-winged, stretched 747-X with room for 550 seats. In addition, Boeing was working with Aerospatiale, British Aerospace, Deutsche Airbus and CASA on what was referred to as the very large commercial transport (VLCT), but this was still at the generic payload/range study stage.

The 747-X and NLA were independent Boeing studies, a common feature amongst the NLA projects being a three-class seating capacity of around 630 passengers (with planned growth to 750 in stretched versions), a range in excess of 14,500km (7,800 nautical miles) and a take-off field length of under 3,350m (11,000ft). Other concerns included emergency cabin evacuation, (particularly on the double-deck aircraft with seating for up to 18 abreast), airport manœuvrability, and compatibility with existing 747 gates. This made it almost certain that any NLA version would have folding wingtips to allow sufficient span to meet take-off field length requirements and climb/cruise targets. A 79m span was the largest achievable without the need for a fold, 83m being manageable with a fold to fit existing facilities. The baseline NLA had a double-deck layout with accommodation for 624 passengers in a three-class layout, with 18 abreast in Economy. The constant-section fuselage would be 76m long and the gross take-off weight would be about 635,600kg. This aircraft would need the full 83m-span wing to meet the 14,500km-range requirement, and new engines would need to be developed with a least 95,000lb (422kN) thrust. Two variations on this layout were an alternative double-deck with a shorter 71.6m fuselage seating up to 584 passengers, and a single-deck version 74.5m long which could seat 627 in three classes with 15 abreast in Economy. This latter scheme resembled a proposed 777 stretch, but with a new wing and four engines. Another option based on 777 wing and fuselage design features was proposed with a new double-deck forward section (41), effectively creating a 747 lookalike with seating for about 630 passengers. The 747-X was seen as the least likely option because it was about 30% longer than the 747-400, which could make it

too long to go round corners. The cost of stretching the fuselage, providing a new wing and effecting structural modifications would make it virtually as expensive as a new design.

Meanwhile, the VLCT twelve-month studies starting in January 1993 were focused on a double-deck 600-seater and a range of 13,000km (7,000nm), although it was not expected to define a configuration apart from outline dimensions. The VLCT was seen as such a large and expensive programme to launch that there were definite advantages in spreading the risks across Europe and the USA. Although its European partners were working with Boeing, Airbus Industrie was independently studying an ultra-high-capacity transport (UHCT) aircraft.

By September, when the 1,000th 747 was rolled off the Everett production-line, developments of the aircraft were having to compete for company finance with the 777, 737-X and, later, 767ER-X projects. The final decision was, as always, influenced by the needs and priorities of the airlines, which at that time appeared to be for greater capacity. The 747 was the only Boeing jet airliner not to have been stretched, and previous experience had shown that this was a cost-effective way to satisfy market needs before a completely new type was required, and often sold in greater numbers than the original aircraft. Having decided that a 747 stretch could be viable, after discussions with the airline consultative group, the fuselage extension was set at 7.1m, split equally fore and aft of the wing, the forward section also including an extension of the upper deck. This length increase would allow seating for another 70 passengers, taking a typical three-class layout to around 490 seats. Overall length would increase from the existing 71m to 78.1m.

To accommodate the increase in weight, the wings, undercarriage and other load-bearing structures would require strengthening, which would first be applied to the gross-weight-increase aircraft, followed by any airframe stretch. Following the market studies, a target MGTOW of 414,000kg was identified, compared with 393,750kg for the heaviest 747-400; the Increased Gross Weight aircraft would be

Above: In June 1990 Air India ordered four 747-400s. Air India 747-437 VT-ESM (c/n 27078) was the first to be delivered, on 4 August 1993. *Air India*

externally identical to the 747-400. Depending upon the airlines' needs, the new version would either have the range increased by 300 nautical miles (550km) to nearly 13,900km, or carry an additional payload of 22,000lb. In addition to putting more fuel in the tailplane, Boeing found extra room for fuel in the forward lower cargo compartment located against the wing front spar; these spaces would allow the carriage of a further 11,300 litres of fuel.

Following flight-testing of the phase 1 PIP modifications, it was found that the re-profiled dorsal section of the lower leading-edge of the fin produced a 0.5% reduction in drag, worth around $60,000 annually in saved fuel. The slowing of the transfer of fuel from the tailplane tanks to improve trim-drag was not embodied as the benefits did not justify the changes. The PIP increases gross weight by 2,270kg and provides either a 180km increase in range or a 1,600kg additional payload.

By October 1993 talks between Boeing and the Airbus partner companies in Europe over collaboration on a possible VLCT were making good progress, the prime factor being to determine if there was sufficient market to justify the risk; it was believed that a 400- to 500-seat aircraft would be needed by the airlines by 2010. A second factor was whether the aircraft could be developed technically, and

a third whether the parties could establish a successful business relationship. Boeing would also have to be able to satisfy the needs of its customers, and the consortium would need complementary skills to keep costs down and provide the right product. In operational terms the new large airliner could add to delays at airports, instead of reducing them — a critical problem could be wake vortex, which might cause such an increase in separation on approach that, even with more passengers, the new large aircraft could result in a lower airport capacity overall; such aircraft might also have a longer runway-occupancy time after landing, requiring even greater separation. These restrictions would apply not only to the VLCT, but to all the Boeing 747 growth projects.

At the delivery of the 1,000th 747 on 14 October 1993 to Singapore Airlines, SIA's deputy chairman confirmed its interest in a 600- to 800-seat very large commercial transport for service entry around 1998, although Boeing thought an eight-year timescale might be more realistic, as it would have been unwise to launch such a programme during the economic downturn which pertained at the time.

By March 1994, Boeing had begun designing a new wing for the 747 stretch, known as the 747-X and to be powered by four engines in the

75,000lb (333kN) thrust bracket. Rolls-Royce was expected to offer the Trent 700, GE an uprated CF6-80E1 or derated GE90, and P&W a PW4000 derivative. The 747-X was planned with a 6m fuselage stretch, giving room for up to 80 more passengers, as an interim answer to the NLA requirement.

Adoption of the re-winged aircraft would delay the NLA well into the next century, as the 747-X and the VLA development could not both be funded at the same time, but the VLCT studies were continuing with the European partners. Studies on stretching the 747 airframe had indicated that fuel capacity would be limited with the current wing, resulting in range being about the same as the 747-200, which was not acceptable to the airlines. Using experience gained with the design of the 777 wing, the new wing for the 747-X would have a more advanced, supercritical airfoil with reduced sweepback and, as a result, a lighter structure. This would allow a Mach 0.84 cruise, and the longer span would give improved payload/range and take-off performance, while the greater area would permit a higher cruise capability and low approach speeds. The integral tanks in the new wing would provide a total fuel capacity of about 250,000 litres (66,000gal US). A completely new wing centre-section would be designed to accommodate the new wing, and the fuselage plugs would be fore and aft, with the forward plug adding room on both decks.

Meanwhile, as the VLCT studies progressed in Europe, Airbus Industrie was invited to join as an advisor on marketing and customer requirements to the European group, the timing of the studies being extended to mid-1995.

In early 1994 Boeing announced an update of the flight-management system (FMS) software which would allow airlines to begin using elements of the Future Air Navigation System (FANS) in 1995. FANS is an internationally-agreed next-generation system for communications, navigation, surveillance and air-traffic management, based on satellite

Above: In October 1990 VARIG ordered six CF6-80C2-powered 747-400s on lease from ILFC, but these were disposed of in August 1994, the long-haul routes being flown thereafter by MD-11s. Boeing 747-475 PP-VPI (c/n 24896; l/n 855) was delivered on 31 May 1991, and is seen taking-off from Everett. This aircraft joined Air New Zealand as ZK-SUH in November 1994. *Boeing*

datalinks. Benefits include reduced separation on airways, more flexible tracks, enhanced safety and reduced arrival and departure delays. The launch airline was QANTAS, with early orders received from Air India, Air New Zealand, Cathay Pacific, Kuwait Airways, Thai International and Cargolux.

By late 1994 Boeing had finalised the design of the proposed NLA, with an upper deck running the full length of the aircraft. It had nothing in common with the 747, being aimed at a totally-new high-capacity market requirement. MGTOW would be about 454,000kg, requiring a six-post main undercarriage, and producing such a large aircraft presented many challenges. The 747 stretch derivatives were still being included in Boeing's plans, to meet ill-defined market requirements. In March 1995, British Airways made public its plans for a higher-capacity fleet to help reduce congestion at London Heathrow; the airline wanted a 500-seat 747 stretch to be in service by 1999, and was looking for a 600-seat NLA to be available within a decade.

In March 1995 Boeing returned to a 747 derivative instead of a new design for the NLA initiative, the likely layout being a stretched fuselage for 500 to 600 passengers, followed by a further stretch to give an 800-seat capacity, and a new wing based on 777 technology. It was quite clear that there was not a market for both the NLA and VLCT; without a definite need, even a company the size of Boeing would be threatened by the huge costs and use of resources.

In mid-1995 the European partners pulled out of the VLCT, but Boeing continued with its own studies on the NLA, the two most likely designs being the 747-500X and 747-600X, with an estimated market for up to 500 aircraft by 2010. The 747-500X would be a 6m stretch of the 747-400 with a three-class layout for 530 passengers and a range of 12,950km (7,000nm). The 747-600X was expected to seat more than 600 passengers in a three-class layout, with up to 800 in a high-density layout over shorter ranges. This version was expected to be 18m longer than the 747-400, with a wingspan of 79m — the largest possible for existing facilities without resorting to a folding wing. Meanwhile Airbus had started its own studies, based around the double-deck A3XX.

As part of its evidence at the inquiry into the expansion of London Heathrow, including the proposed new Terminal 5, BA mooted the introduction of a 700-seat 747 development by the turn of the century. Boeing confirmed that it was considering giving the go-ahead in 1996 to the 747-500X, with an increased range of between 14,500 and 14,800km, and the 747-600X, with seating for between 550 and 700 passengers. The planned versions would have new wings and engines based upon the 777, and the 747-600X would have an overall length of 86m (280ft), some 15m longer than the 747-400. As well as an increased payload, the 747-600X would have a range of just over 12,950km (7,000nm), a modest increase over the 747-400. The 747-500X would have a slight increase in length over the 747-400, due to the longer centre-section needed to accommodate the increased wing-chord at the root, and would in effect be a replacement for the earlier aircraft. Derivatives of the 747-400 were now favoured by Boeing because of their lower costs, and the airlines welcomed the commonality with their existing fleets. BA was particularly interested in the higher-capacity 747-600X, with its small but useful increase in range.

For an update and feedback from the airline advisory group, Boeing called a further meeting at Everett in November 1995, with a view to setting a launch date in 1996. Operators attending the meeting included British Airways, Cathay Pacific, QANTAS and Singapore Airlines — the latter being the largest operator of the 747-400. The plan was to produce the new variants alongside the 747-400 in the existing facilities at Everett to save the costs associated with building a new factory. The proposals were in direct competition with the Airbus A3XX.

In February 1996, Boeing revealed that it was close to getting launch orders for the 747-600X from BA, Lufthansa and Singapore Airlines, and in April a meeting of the 14-airline advisory group helped define the requirements for — and configurations of — the derivatives. The timetable was for the launch of the high-density 747-600X at the end of the year,

Above: To keep its crews current, SIA uses a 747-400 for crew training at Changi Airport, Singapore. *Singapore Airlines*

followed by the long-range 747-500X six months later. The new wing was to be scaled up by around 30% from the 777, but would not require major strengthening due to the wing-bending relief provided by the outboard engines. The 777's engines were seen as too large, and, as Boeing wanted to avoid the introduction of new types, consideration was given to the CF6-80E1, PW4168 and Trent 700 being used on the Airbus A330. The expected range of both new 747 versions had increased slightly, to 15,000-15,700km for the 747-500X, with a MGTOW of between 590,000kg and 680,000kg, and to around 13,300km for the 747-600X. The market for these larger-capacity jetliners was predicted to reach 1,588 aircraft by 2015, with major sales expected in the then fast-growing Asian sector.

Once Boeing had decided to rule out a derivative engine, GE and Pratt & Whitney, in an effort to reduce costs, joined forces in May 1996 to develop a new engine for the planned 747 improvement programme, the thrust range covering 72,000 to 84,000lb (320-374kN) with service entry due for 2000. The size and range of the aircraft had outgrown the A330 engines,

and the choice was between derivatives of the 777 powerplants and new types, although Rolls-Royce was planning to offer a version of the Trent 800. The key performance goals of the engines were to reduce operating costs by 10% with low noise, while achieving 777 reliability levels.

By mid-1996 the airlines were requesting more range from the high-capacity 747-600X, increasing their requirement to 14,060km (7,600nm) to give an advantage over the sometimes payload-restricted 747-400. MGTOW would be raised by 45,500kg to 513,000kg due to the additional fuel. Service entry of the 747-600X was planned for the end of 2000, with the 747-500X to follow a year later.

Boeing was preparing to seek board approval for the new aircraft in July 1996, but expected the development timescale to be extended by over a year due to the incorporation of new technology requested by the airline advisory group. If board approval was granted, then formal launch of both variants was expected in September. Notwithstanding the extended development period which would be required, the airlines were keen to have the latest technology incorporated in the new aircraft, including full fly-by-wire (FBW) and the latest information-management systems, including automatic checklists and electrical load management. The airlines were prepared to wait an extra two years for the full development programme, although this would put an additional strain on Boeing's finances. The gross weight for both versions was now expected to be around 545,000kg, and, despite the introduction of new technology, service entry was still planned for December 2000. Boeing had initially resisted the inclusion of FBW, as it wanted the new versions to be treated as derivatives of the 747-400. However, the decision was taken to make use of the 777 technology and to certificate as a new type.

The hope was still to launch the programme formally at the Farnborough Air Show in September 1996, the aircraft on offer having been refined to the 747-500X carrying up to 487 passengers in a three-class arrangement over a 15,100km (8,200 nautical mile) range with a fuselage length of 79m, and the 747-600X carrying 546 passengers up to 13,875km with a length of 85m. Thai Airways was considering signing an MoU for up to six of the new aircraft, pending Thai Government approval for an earlier fleet-modernisation programme.

Further refinement took place in late July, when Boeing announced a reduction in size of the -500X and a further increase in range of the -600X, following further discussions with the airline consultative group. The fuselage length of the -500X was shortened by 3m to 76m, yielding a range increase from 15,080km to 16,100km, but with passenger capacity reduced from 487 to 462. The -600X had its range increased by 460km to 14,340km (7,750 nautical miles) with a three-class layout of 548 passengers; MGTOW was revised to 538,440kg, with zero-fuel and maximum landing weights at 358,660 and 383,630kg respectively. The two types were to share a common wing with a span of 76.6m and no winglets.

Because of the increased weights, major changes were to be made to the undercarriage. Both versions were to have two wing-mounted

six-wheel main legs and two fuselage-mounted four-wheel units, providing 20 main wheels, and all the main units would be steerable. The nosegear would have four wheels mounted on the same axis. Approach speed was to be reduced by 7kt (13km/h) to keep the landing-roll the same as the 747-400's at maximum landing-weight. The avionics systems were to be based on 777 experience.

The 747-500X and -600X were to have their hydraulic systems reduced from four to three due to lack of space in the outboard engine pylons. The left and right systems would be driven by the relevant inboard engine, and would be used to power the FCS. The third, central system would be bleed-air driven, providing power for the undercarriage, brakes and flaps. In addition to an APU, a ram-air turbine (RAT) would be installed to satisfy certification requirements for emergency power-sources.

Boeing was by now defining an engine power requirement of 77,000lb (343kN) with growth to 80,000lb (356kN). The GE and P&W joint venture was planning to offer an all-new engine with a 2.75-2.8m fan. GE would be responsible for the HP compressor and turbine as well as the combustors, and P&W for the fan and LP compressor and turbine. The GE-P&W alliance was planning final assembly of the GP7000 engine programme at the East Hartford, Connecticut, plant of P&W. The initial engine was to be the 76,000lb (338kN) GP7176, with certification expected at the end of 1999. Rolls-Royce was planning to supply the 80,000lb (356kN) Trent 900, with a 2.8m-diameter fan, and the combustor from the Trent 895. The IP and HP compressors would be scaled down from those in the 895, and a new, five-stage LP turbine would reduce loadings on the IP and HP turbines.

With Boeing having settled the baseline specification for the new airliners, they were ready to offer to potential customers. However, with a week to go to the planned launch, Boeing was experiencing difficulty in confirming sufficient airline support, partly due to the price tag of $230 million for the 747-600X as compared with $165 million for the 747-400. Before seeking board approval, Boeing had hoped to have signed MoUs, in particular from BA, Cathay Pacific, Malaysian Airlines, Singapore Airlines and Thai International, each for an initial six aircraft, mainly of the 747-600X version. United was reported to be interested in seven aircraft and Japan Airlines a further five. However, the airlines were reluctant to be rushed, since the baseline specifications had only been established for about a month and they needed time for evaluation.

To confuse the marketplace still further, Boeing announced its NLA at the Farnborough Show as the 747-700X, with a three-class layout for 650 passengers, in direct competition with the proposed Airbus A3XX. The -700X would have the same wing as the -500X and -600X, with a wider, high-capacity fuselage and increased upper-deck capacity, and be ready for service in 2007, about four years after the A3XX. The massive development costs could be shared across the three aircraft programmes. It was also announced at the Farnborough Show that Malaysian Airlines and Thai Airways had committed to up to 18 747-500X/600X.

By the end of September, Boeing received authority from its board to offer the 747-500X and -600X to the airlines. Lufthansa, as a prospective launch customer, was critical of the latest design proposals, which in effect left little in common with the 747-400, opening the field for competing proposals with the A3XX. Due to pressure from the airlines, the new cockpit was to have full fly-by-wire control, and new engines were being specified, pushing up the cost of the aircraft.

During October 1996, Boeing was making the final adjustments to the 747-500X and -600X specifications following further discussions with potential customers, ready for a programme launch in early 1997. The decision had been made to make wider use of 777 systems rather than those of the 747-400, making the aircraft more attractive to 777 operators. Amongst the changes was an increase in wingspan to 77.7m (255ft), but the length of the -600X had been reduced slightly, to 84.5m. The plan was still to deliver the first aircraft by December 2000.

Despite all its efforts, on 20 January 1997 Boeing announced the shelving of the

747-500X/600X programme to concentrate on developments of the 767 and 777. It was unable to make an effective business case due to the apparently small size of the market, leaving the field open to Airbus, although there were possibilities of further improvements to the basic 747-400. By late February these were evolving into an initial version known as the 747-400 Increased Gross Weight (IGW), which would offer a slight increase in range, possibly followed by a modest stretch for 60-80 more passengers, but with significantly less range than the 747-400. The 747-400IGW would have MGTOW increased from 397 to 418 tonnes, offering an increase in range of 740km (400nm), to 14,060km. An anticipated drawback was the need for more power from the engines in the region of 63,000-64,000lb (280-285kN) thrust, which could probably not be achieved from the existing engines, and although the GE-P&W alliance was about to break up, this gave a possible application for the GP7000. The stretched version, with its reduced range, could be of interest to the Asian airlines for high-density regional services.

In mid-1997, Boeing began to step up work on the 747-400IGW and the proposed stretch, and was requesting a 65,000lb (289kN)-thrust engine which would allow a MGTOW of 940,000lb (427,000kg) and the same range as the 747-400 for the stretched version with a 10% reduction in operating costs. The plans were in fact reverting to the original 1993 concepts, and featured the same characteristics, systems and cockpit as the existing 747-400, to allow common crew ratings. The wing would not be changed, the -500X and -600X having become too ambitious, and the simple stretch to the fuselage would be about 2.8m in fore and aft plugs, providing room for 80-100 more passengers.

By September 1997, the 747-400IGW had become the -400X, with a gross weight of 426,000kg and a range increase of around 1,800km, to 15,200km, while the -400X Stretch would be able to carry 485 passengers over similar ranges to the 747-400. Two further options being considered included a wing-root insert and a wingspan fillet, to create the 747-400RI and -400RI Stretch. To accommodate the broader root-chord of the wing, the fuselage centre-section would have a modest stretch increasing seating capacity by 15, to 435 and 500 respectively. The -400RI would have a range of nearly 15,400km, and the -400RI Stretch would have a range of 14,000km with a gross weight of 472,000kg. A fifth hybrid option being discussed with airlines was to take the short upper-deck fuselage of the 747-200 and attach to it the stronger wing of the 747-400 Freighter, as a direct competitor to the Airbus A340-600. This version of the 747, known as the -400 Plus, would be able to carry between 355 and 380 passengers over 14,800km. It would not require new engines, the MGTOW going up to between 399,500kg and 413,100kg but kept to a minimum through the use of new materials. The aircraft would in effect be the 747-400F airframe filled with passengers. Studies continued, to determine whether more power would be required, and whether the undercarriage would need strengthening, both of which were being resisted by the airlines.

As a result of pressure from QANTAS for the launch of the 747-400X to allow the airline to overcome payload restrictions on the routes from Australia to Europe and the USA, the Boeing board approved the offer of the 747-400IGW with a MGTOW of 413,140kg and a range up to 14,245km (7,700nm). There would be local structural strengthening around the centre-section, wing to fuselage joint, wing, flaps and undercarriage, the latter being most critical from a delivery point of view. The wing-root inserts would offer a range of 15,200km and form the basis of a stretched version with 485 seats. First deliveries were planned for the latter part of 2000.

With the 747-400IGW on formal offer to the airlines but not committed to development, in early 1998 Boeing revised the proposals for the future growth version to a 500-seater known as the 747-400Y Stretch. This would utilise many of the structural changes developed for the 747-400IGW, but the fuselage would be stretched by 9.4m and have a wing-root extension of 2.3m, to an overall span of 69m. The additional room in the wing would allow enough fuel for the full load of passengers to be

carried over ranges of 13,875km (7,500nm), the MGTOW increasing to over 454,000kg. This new offering coincided with Airbus's delaying the entry into service of the 555-seat A3XX until the third quarter of 2004, and Boeing hoped to capture part of that market. Power was to come from the R-R Trent 900 and the GE/P&W GP7000. All these new high-density passenger airliners were aimed primarily at the Asian market, which in 1998 showed a serious downturn in the economy, delaying early commitments from that region.

Despite delays, which caused QANTAS to buy secondhand 747-400s surplus to the Asian market, in mid-1998 Boeing announced the firm specification for the 747 development known as the 747-400X, with a service introduction in less than three years as the -400ER. The MGTOW was increased to 409,500kg (910,000lb), and a range of 14,260km (7,700nm) — later growing to 14,800km (8,000nm) — was possible. The new version would be a minimum change from the existing 747-400 but would have strengthened main landing-gear with radial tyres and new wheels, and local structural strengthening to the nosewheel bay, tail, outboard wing (taken from the -400F), and parts of the fuselage around the centre section. Additional fuel would be available in one or two auxiliary 12,040-litre fuel tanks at the rear of the forward cargo hold. The systems would require minor modifications to accommodate the gross weight and fuel volume increases. Boeing was offering the 747-400X as an alternative to the smaller-capacity and yet-to-be-launched 777-200X, and also in competition with the Airbus A340-500 and -600. A simple 747-400X stretch seating 70 more passengers would retain the -400ER wing, but would need engines with 65,000lb (290kN) thrust, offering a 12,950km range, but would lack the wing inserts of the -400Y.

With many of the Asian carriers looking to defer — and in some cases cancel — orders, this was probably not the best time to be launching an improved version of the 747; Boeing therefore delayed the launch decision of the 747-400X to the end of 1998, putting first deliveries to the end of 2001 — a year later than planned. As the year-end approached, the Asian economic crisis became worse, and Boeing itself had a difficult year with delivery delays across all its civil programmes, caused by resources being stretched too far. While deliveries were improving, the market for long-range airliners was diminishing.

At the Paris Show in June 1999, in response to a perceived interest from the key Asian carriers, Boeing revived its plans for the 747-400X Stretch. The 500-seat aircraft would have a 9.2m fuselage extension and 4.6m increase in wingspan achieved by installing root extensions. This would require overall structural strengthening with new main landing-gear and increased-thrust engines. Using some aerodynamic changes to the wing, flight-tested on an Asiana aircraft, range could be increased to between 15,000km (8,150nm) and 16,000km with 450 to 500 passengers and a MGTOW of 1,043,000lb (473.5t). Additional fuel could be housed in the enlarged wing. To ensure adequate lateral stability in the cruise as well as improved directional control during landing and take-off, changes were to be made to the vertical and horizontal tail-surfaces.

Boeing has gone through a very difficult period over the last decade, with studies on 747-400 improvements using up considerable engineering resources and large sums of money, and (at the time of writing) no firm decision to do anything but continue building the existing 747-400, albeit in reducing numbers. By working with its potential customers, Boeing probably gained more feedback than was really needed since each airline has its own unique product and requirements. The airlines wanted new technology at no extra cost, with the conflicting requirement for commonality in terms of operation and support. Boeing's responses were also being driven by the competitive products of Airbus Industrie, which help keep prices keen. With no firm decision by Boeing, it appears that the future large-aircraft market may be dominated by Airbus — a state which will not be acceptable to Boeing, if it can make a viable business case to build a competitor.

Above: At the end of 1998 SAA took delivery of two ex-PAL 747-400s, one of which was 747-4F6 ZS-SBK (c/n 28959), which was delivered on 30 December 1998. It is seen turning on to the runway at London Heathrow in July 1999 in the airline's new colour scheme. *Nick Granger*

APPENDICES
I. Specification

NB: P&W = PW4056;   GE = CF6-80C2;   R-R = RB211-524G/H

Dimensions
Wingspan	64.31m (211ft)
Length	70.66m (231ft 10in)
Height	19.33m (63ft 5in)
Wing chord at root	16.56m (54ft 4in)
Wing area	511sq m (5,500sq ft)
Wing aspect ratio	7.0
Wheel track	11m (36ft 1in)
Wheelbase	25.6m (84ft)
Cabin length	57m (187ft)
Cabin width	6.13m (20ft 1½ in)
Cabin height	2.54m (8ft 4in)

Weights
Operating weight empty (P&W)	180,985kg (399,000lb)
(GE)	181,030kg (399,100lb)
(R-R)	182,255kg (401,800lb)
Maximum take-off weight	394,625kg (870,000lb)
Maximum zero fuel weight	242,670kg (535,000lb)
Maximum landing weight	285,765kg (630,000lb)

Performance
Maximum cruise speed	986km/h (507kt; 611mph) = Mach 0.85
Approach speed	284km/h (146kt; 176mph)
Initial cruise altitude	10,030m (32,900ft)
Maximum cruise altitude	13,725m (45,000ft)
Take-off field length* (P&W)	3,322m (10,900ft)
(GE)	3,322m (10,900ft)
(R-R)	3,352m (11,000ft)
Landing field length	2,072m (6,800ft)
Typical range (P&W)	13,269km (7,165nm)
(GE)	13,390km (7,230nm)
(R-R)	13,149km (7,100nm)

*at sea level

Above: Line No 767 — JAL 747-446 JA8073 (c/n 24425 — first flew on 26 January 1990. It is seen soon after turning on finals to Hong Kong Kai Tak in April 1998. *Author*

II. Production

L/n	C/n	Model	Airline	Identity	Delivered
696	23719	451	Northwest Airlines	N661US	8.12.89
700	23817	430	Lufthansa	D-ABVB	30.9.89
705	23814	467	Cathay Pacific Airways	B-HOO	26.9.88
708	23720	451	Northwest Airlines	N662US	13.3.89
715	23818	451	Northwest Airlines	N663US	26.1.89
717	24061	412	Singapore Airlines	9V-SMA	29.3.89
721	23819	451	Northwest Airlines	N664US	28.4.89
722	24062	412	Singapore Airlines	9V-SMB	18.3.89
723	23816	430	Lufthansa	D-ABVA	23.5.89
725	23999	406	KLM	PH-BFA	18.5.89
726	23820	451	Northwest Airlines	N665US	1.9.89
727	23908	436	British Airways	G-BNLA	30.6.89
728	23815	467	Cathay Pacific Airways	B-HOP	8.6.89
729	24198	4B5	Korean Air	HL7477	13.6.89
730	23909	436	British Airways	G-BNLB	31.7.89
731	24354	438	QANTAS	VH-OJA	17.8.89
732	24000	406	KLM	PH-BFB	20.6.89
733	24322	422	United Airlines	N171UA	30.6.89
734	23910	436	British Airways	G-BNLC	21.7.89
735	23982	406 Combi	KLM	PH-BFC	1.9.89
736	24063	412	Singapore Airlines	9V-SMC	11.7.89
737	24001	406 Combi	KLM	PH-BFD	29.9.89
738	24315	4H6 Combi	Malaysian Airlines	9M-MHL	17.11.89
739	24199	4B5	Korean Air	HL7478	28.7.89
740	24363	422	United Airlines	N172UA	21.8.89
741	24154	4B3	UTA; to Air France	F-GEXA	22.9.89
742	23821	451	Northwest Airlines	N666US	18.8.89
743	24346	4J6 Combi	Air China	B-2456	13.10.89
744	23911	436	British Airways	G-BNLD	5.9.89
745	24405	4H6 Combi	Malaysian Airlines	9M-MHM	6.10.89
746	24373	438	QANTAS	VH-OJB	21.9.89

Above: Line No 815 — Air New Zealand 747-419 ZK-NBT (c/n 24855) — was delivered on 31 October 1990, and is seen in the airline's old livery at London Gatwick in March 1991. *Nick Granger*

Above: Line No 829 — BA 747-436 G-BNLR (c/n 24447) — was delivered on 15 January 1991, and is seen with 'Rendezvous' fin colours on approach to Hong Kong Kai Tak in April 1998. *Author*

747	24285	430 Combi	Lufthansa	D-ABTA	19.9.89
748	24200	4B5	Korean Air	HL7479	13.9.89
749	24286	430 Combi	Lufthansa	D-ABTB	22.12.89
751	24406	438	QANTAS	VH-OJC	14.10.89
753	24047	436	British Airways	G-BNLE	15.10.89
754	24287	430 Combi	Lufthansa	D-ABTC	3.2.90
755	24064	412	Singapore Airlines	9V-SMD	1.11.89
756	24386	419	Air New Zealand	ZK-NBS	14.12.89
757	24288	430	Lufthansa	D-ABVC	26.10.89
758	24423	446	Japan Airlines	JA8071	25.1.90
759	24380	422	United Airlines	N173UA	8.12.89
760	24424	446	Japan Airlines	JA8072	25.1.90
761	24065	412	Singapore Airlines	9V-SME	13.12.89
762	24381	422	United Airlines	N174UA	20.1.90
763	24201	406 Combi	KLM	PH-BFE	24.1.90
764	24481	438	QANTAS	VH-OJD	16.1.90
765	24482	438	QANTAS	VH-OJE	31.1.90
766	24309	409	China Airlines	B-161	8.2.90
767	24425	446	Japan Airlines	JA8073	19.2.90
768	24426	446	Japan Airlines	JA8074	26.2.90
769	24458	4D7	Thai Airways International	HS-TGH	21.2.90
770	24202	406 Combi	KLM	PH-BFF	23.2.90
771	24631	467	Cathay Pacific Airways	B-HOR	9.2.90
773	24048	436	British Airways	G-BNLF	28.2.90
774	24049	436	British Airways	G-BNLG	27.2.90
775	24347	4J6 Combi	Air China	B-2458	27.2.90
777	24459	4D7	Thai Airways International	HS-TGJ	22.3.90
778	24310	409	China Airlines	B-162	27.3.90
779	24050	436	British Airways	G-BNLH	28.3.90
780	24427	446	Japan Airlines	JA8075	30.3.90
781	24483	438	QANTAS	VH-OJF	8.4.90
782	24517	406	KLM	PH-BFG	11.4.90
783	24518	406 Combi	KLM	PH-BFH	26.4.90
784	24051	436	British Airways	G-BNLI	21.4.90
785	24715	430	Lufthansa	D-ABTD	27.4.90
786	24740	430	Lufthansa/Condor	D-ABVD	15.5.90
787	24741	430	Lufthansa	D-ABVE	4.5.90
788	24850	467	Cathay Pacific Airways	B-HOS	11.5.90
789	24052	436	British Airways	G-BNLJ	23.5.90

790	24053	436	British Airways	G-BNLK	25.5.90
791	24066	412	Singapore Airlines	9V-SMF	19.6.90
792	24348	4J6 Combi	Air China	B-2460	21.6.90
793	24619	4B5	Korean Air	HL7480	27.6.90
794	24054	436	British Airways	G-BNLL	14.6.90
795	24055	436	British Airways	G-BNLM	28.6.90
796	24761	430	Lufthansa/Condor	D-ABVF	6.7.90
797	24777	446	Japan Airlines	JA8076	10.7.90
798	24784	446	Japan Airlines	JA8077	10.7.90
799	24222	451	Northwest Airlines	N667US	20.7.90
800	24223	451	Northwest Airlines	N668US	26.7.90
801	24779	438	QANTAS	VH-OJG	18.8.90
802	24056	436	British Airways	G-BNLN	27.7.90
803	24224	451	Northwest Airlines	N669US	20.8.90
804	24225	451	Northwest Airlines	N670US	31.8.90
805	24801	481	All Nippon Airways	JA8094	28.8.90

Above: Line No 840 — Air Canada 747-433SCD Combi C-GAGL '341' (c/n 24998) — was delivered on 4 June 1991, and is seen at the holding point at London Heathrow in November 1996. **Author**

806	24382	422	United Airlines	N175UA	16.8.90
807	24806	438	QANTAS	VH-OJH	3.9.90
808	24836	4H6	Malaysian Airlines	9M-MHN	27.9.90
809	24226	412	Singapore Airlines	9V-SMG	27.9.90
811	24383	422	United Airlines	N176UA	19.9.90
812	24833	481	All Nippon Airways	JA8095	10.10.90
813	24851	467	Cathay Pacific Airways	B-HOT	28.9.90
815	24855	419	Air New Zealand	ZK-NBT	31.10.90
816	24730	47C	Japanese Government	JA8091	17.9.91
817	24057	436	British Airways	G-BNLO	25.10.90
819	24384	422	United Airlines	N177UA	8.11.90
820	24385	422	United Airlines	N178UA	8.11.90
821	24870	446	Japan Airlines	JA8078	19.11.90
823	24883	475	Canadian Airlines International	C-GMWW	11.12.90
824	24885	446	Japan Airlines	JA8079	5.12.90
825	24886	446	Japan Airlines	JA8080	12.12.90
826	24887	438	QANTAS	VH-OJI	23.12.90
827	24976	444	South African Airways	ZS-SAV	19.1.91

828	24058	436	British Airways	G-BNLP	17.12.90
829	24447	436	British Airways	G-BNLR	15.1.91
830	24621	4B5	Korean Air	HL7481	31.1.91
831	24227	412	Singapore Airlines	9V-SMH	24.1.91
832	24920	481	All Nippon Airways	JA8096	5.2.91
833	24993	4D7	Thai Airways International	HS-TGK	31.1.91
834	24925	467	Cathay Pacific Airways	B-HOU	18.1.91
835	24974	438	QANTAS	VH-OJJ	21.2.91
836	24969	428	Air France	F-GITA	28.2.91
837	24895	475	Canadian Airlines International	C-FCRA	15.2.91
838	24975	412	Singapore Airlines	9V-SMI	25.2.91
839	24731	47C	Japanese Government	JA8092	18.11.91
840	24998	433 Combi	Air Canada	C-GAGL	4.6.91
841	24629	436	British Airways	G-BNLS	13.3.91
842	24630	436	British Airways	G-BNLT	19.3.91
843	24990	428 Combi	Air France	F-GITB	5.4.91

Above: Line No 894 — QANTAS 747438 VH-OJO (c/n 25544) *City of Toowoomba* — was delivered on 21 May 1992, and is seen at Sydney in December 1992. *Author*

844	25213	446D	Japan Airlines	JA8083	10.10.91
845	25045	430	Lufthansa	D-ABVH	3.4.91
846	24966	430 Combi	Lufthansa	D-ABTE	13.4.91
847	25046	430	Lufthansa	D-ABVK	19.4.91
848	24967	430 Combi	Lufthansa	D-ABTF	23.4.91
849	25082	467	Cathay Pacific Airways	B-HOV	24.4.91
850	25086	406 Combi	KLM	PH-BFI	5.5.91
851	25064	446	Japan Airlines	JA8081	13.5.91
852	25068	412	Singapore Airlines	9V-SMJ	21.5.91
853	25205	4B5	Korean Air	HL7482	22.5.91
854	25087	406 Combi	KLM	PH-BFK	21.5.91
855	24896	475	VARIG	PP-VPI	31.5.91
856	25047	430 Combi	Lufthansa	D-ABTH	5.6.91
857	25067	438	QANTAS	VH-OJK	20.6.91
858	25126	4H6	Malaysian; to QANTAS	9M-MHO	10.6.91
859	25127	412	Singapore Airlines	9V-SMK	25.6.91
860	25128	412	Singapore Airlines	9V-SML	20.6.91
861	25152	444	South African Airways	ZS-SAW	28.6.91
862	25074	433 Combi	Air Canada	C-GAGM	16.7.91

Above: Line No 928 — ANA 747-481 JA8958 (c/n 25641) — was delivered on 11 August 1992, and is seen turning on to final approach to Hong Kong Kai Tak in November 1993. *Asian Aviation Photography*

863	25135	481	All Nippon Airways	JA8097	11.7.91
864	24155	4B3 Combi	UTA; to Air France	F-GEXB	26.7.91
865	25151	438	QANTAS	VH-OJL	26.7.91
866	25158	422	United Airlines	N179UA	31.7.91
867	25224	422	United Airlines	N180UA	30.7.91
868	25075	433 Combi	Air Canada	C-GAGN	30.8.91
869	24311	409	China Airlines	B-163	14.8.91
870	25207	481	All Nippon Airways	JA8098	21.8.91
871	25212	446	Japan Airlines	JA8082	27.8.91
872	25238	428 Combi	Air France	F-GISA	17.9.91
873	25211	467	Cathay Pacific Airways	B-HOW	20.8.91
874	25275	4B5	Korean Air	HL7483	11.9.91
875	25245	438	QANTAS	VH-OJM	20.9.91
876	25260	446	Japan Airlines	JA8085	24.9.91
877	24955	467	Cathay Pacific Airways	B-HOX	25.9.91
879	25214	446D	Japan Airlines	JA8084	14.10.91
880	25405	48E Combi	Asiana Airlines	HL7413	1.11.91
881	25278	422	United Airlines	N181UA	23.10.91
882	25279	422	United Airlines	N182UA	24.10.91
883	25315	438	QANTAS	VH-OJN	10.11.91
884	25302	428 Combi	Air France	F-GISB	8.11.91
885	25308	446	Japan Airlines	JA8086	11.11.91
887	25351	467	Cathay Pacific Airways	B-HOY	22.11.91
888	25356	406	KLM	PH-BFL	5.12.91
889	25344	428	Air France	F-GITC	9.12.91
890	25366	4D7	Thai Airways International	HS-TGL	12.12.91
891	25292	481D	All Nippon Airways	JA8099	13.1.92
892	25452	48E Combi	Asiana Airlines	HL7414	7.1.92
893	26392	4B5	Korean Air	HL7484	28.1.92
894	25544	438	QANTAS	VH-OJO	24.5.92
895	25406	436	British Airways	G-BNLU	28.1.92
896	26373	406 Combi	KLM	PH-BFM	14.2.92
897	26346	446	Japan Airlines	JA8087	18.2.92
898	26425	430	Lufthansa	D-ABVL	20.2.92
899	25599	428 Combi	Air France	F-GISC	18.2.92
900	25427	436	British Airways	G-BNLV	20.2.92
901	25600	428	Air France	F-GITD	19.2.92

902	26341	446	Japan Airlines	JA8088	24.2.92
903	25432	436	British Airways	G-BNLW	5.3.92
904	25879	4J6	Air China	B-2464	20.3.92
905	26342	446	Japan Airlines	JA8089	11.3.92
906	25601	428	Air France	F-GITE	18.3.92
907	26347	446D	Japan Airlines	JA8090	26.3.92
908	25435	436	British Airways	G-BNLX	3.4.92
909	25602	428	Air France	F-GITF	7.4.92
910	26426	430	Lufthansa/Brunei	D-ABVM	17.4.92
911	25379	422	United Airlines	N183UA	20.4.92
912	25422	475	Canadian Airlines International	C-FBCA	22.4.92
913	25380	422	United Airlines	N184UA	1.5.92
914	25639	481D	All Nippon Airways	JA8955	12.5.92
915	26427	430	Lufthansa	D-ABVN	8.5.92
916	25545	438	QANTAS	VH-OJP	28.6.92
917	24956	441	VARIG; to Garuda	PP-VPG	1.6.92
918	26343	446	Japan Airlines	JA8901	1.6.92
919	25395	422	United Airlines	N185UA	1.6.92
920	25640	481D	All Nippon Airways	JA8956	9.6.92
921	26547	412	Singapore Airlines	9V-SMM	11.6.92
922	26395	4B5	Korean Air	HL7485	23.6.92
923	26548	412	Singapore Airlines	9V-SMN	16.6.92
924	25546	438	QANTAS	VH-OJQ	20.9.92
925	25871	467	Cathay Pacific Airways	B-HOZ	22.6.92
926	25880	4J6	Air China	B-2466	6.8.92
927	25642	481D	All Nippon Airways	JA8957	15.7.92
928	25641	481	All Nippon Airways	JA8958	11.8.92
929	26344	446	Japan Airlines	JA8902	19.8.92
930	25872	467	Cathay Pacific Airways	B-HUA	30.7.92
931	26875	422	United Airlines	N186UA	24.8.92
932	27042	4H6	Malaysian Airlines	9M-MPA	27.8.92
933	25605	419	Air New Zealand	ZK-NBU	14.9.92
934	25628	428	Air France	F-GISD	4.9.92
935	26345	446D	Japan Airlines	JA8903	15.9.92
936	25547	438	QANTAS	VH-OJR	18.10.92
937	25873	467	Cathay Pacific Airways	B-HUB	9.10.92
938	25413	406 Combi	KLM	PH-BFO	8.10.92
939	26876	422	United Airlines	N187UA	28.9.92
940	27066	412	Singapore Airlines	9V-SMO	13.10.92
941	26348	446D	Japan Airlines	JA8904	3.11.92
942	27062	45E	EVA Airways	B-16401	2.11.92
943	26637	444	South African Airways	ZS-SAX	27.10.92
944	26877	422	United Airlines	N188UA	4.12.92
945	27093	4D7	Thai Airways International	HS-TGM	4.11.92
946	25777	48E Combi	Asiana Airlines	HL7415	3.12.92
947	27063	45E	EVA Airways	B-16402	10.11.92
948	26349	446D	Japan Airlines	JA8905	1.12.92
949	25874	467	Cathay Pacific Airways	B-HUD	10.12.92
950	26615	4D7	Thai Airways International	HS-TGN	8.12.92
951	26396	4B5	Korean Air	HL7486	12.1.93
952	25646	481D	All Nippon Airways	JA8959	11.1.93
953	27067	412	Singapore Airlines	9V-SMP	22.12.92
954	24312	409	China Airlines	B-164	11.1.93
955	27132	412	Singapore Airlines	9V-SMQ	30.1.93
956	25629	428	Air France; to Royal Air Maroc	F-OGTG	25.1.93
957	25881	4J6	Air China	B-2443	24.2.93
958	26393	4B5	Korean Air	HL7487	9.2.93
959	27090	436	British Airways	G-BNLY	10.2.93
960	25630	428 Combi	Air France	F-GISE	10.2.93
961	26350	446	Japan Airlines	JA8906	1.3.93
962	27133	412	Singapore Airlines	9V-SMR	26.2.93

963	26351	446D	Japan Airlines	JA8907	2.3.93
964	27091	436	British Airways	G-BNLZ	4.3.93
965	25699	4H6	Malaysian Airlines	9M-MPB	1.4.93
966	26878	422	United Airlines	N189UA	23.3.93
967	27092	436	British Airways	G-CIVA	22.3.93
968	25632	428F	Cargolux	LX-ICV	12.9.95
969	26373	406	KLM	PH-BFN	8.4.93
970	27117	467	Cathay Pacific Airways	B-HUE	7.5.93
971	24957	441	VARIG; to Air NZ	PP-VPH	20.4.93
972	25643	481D	All Nippon Airways	JA8960	11.5.93
973	26879	422	United Airlines	N190UA	22.4.93
974	25700	4H6	Malaysian Airlines	9M-MPC	10.5.93
975	25644	481D	All Nippon Airways	JA8961	13.5.93
976	27141	45E (SCD)	EVA Airways	N403EV	10.5.93
977	24313	409	China Airlines (w/o 4.11.93)	B-165	8.6.93
978	26352	446D	Japan Airlines	JA8908	1.6.93
979	25645	481	All Nippon Airways	JA8962	3.6.93
980	26353	446	Japan Airlines	JA8909	7.6.93
981	27134	412	Singapore Airlines	9V-SMS	20.6.93
982	27142	45E (SCD)	EVA Airways	N405EV	15.6.93
983	25778	48E	Asiana; to QANTAS	HL7416	24.6.93
984	26880	422	United Airlines	N191UA	24.6.93
985	26473	451	United Airlines	N105UA	17.6.94
986	26394	4B5	Korean Air	HL7488	27.7.93
987	27078	437	Air India	VT-ESM	4.8.93
988	26474	451	United Airlines	N106UA	25.7.94
989	26881	422	United Airlines	N192UA	2.8.93
990	27137	412	Singapore Airlines	9V-SMT	19.8.93
991	25647	481D	All Nippon Airways	JA8963	31.8.93
992	26374	406	KLM	PH-BFP	1.9.93
993	25869	467	Cathay Pacific Airways	B-HUF	20.8.93
994	27154	45E	EVA Airways	B-16461	16.9.93
995	26638	444	South African Airways	ZS-SAY	5.10.93
996	27163	481D	All Nippon Airways	JA8964	24.3.94
997	25701	4H6	Malaysian Airlines	9M-MPD	5.10.93
998	27173	45E Combi	EVA Airways	B-16462	7.10.93
999	25702	4H6	Malaysian Airlines	9M-MPE	9.11.93
1000	27068	412	Singapore Airlines	9V-SMU	14.10.93
1001	26609	4D7	Thai Airways International	HS-TGO	20.10.93
1002	25866	4R7F	Cargolux	LX-FCV	17.11.93
1003	27164	437	Air India	VT-ESN	12.11.93
1004	27174	45E Combi	EVA Airways	B-16463	3.11.93
1005	27261	4F6	Philippine Airlines	N751PR	19.11.93
1006	25779	48E	Asiana Airlines	HL7417	3.12.93
1007	25870	467	Cathay Pacific Airways	B-HUG	10.12.93
1008	25867	4R7F	Cargolux	LX-GCV	8.12.93
1009	27165	437 Combi	Air India	VT-ESO	10.12.93
1010	27069	412	Singapore Airlines	9V-SMV	22.12.93
1011	25704	4U3	Garuda Indonesian Airways	PK-GSG	14.1.94
1012	27262	4F6	Philippine Airlines	N725PR	21.12.93
1013	27072	4B5	Korean Air	HL7489	18.1.94
1014	27202	406 Combi	KLM	PH-BFR	14.1.94
1015	27178	412	Singapore Airlines	9V-SMW	28.1.94
1016	26062	45E Combi	EVA Airways	B-16465	27.1.94
1017	27043	4H6	Malaysian Airlines	9M-MPF	31.1.94
1018	25811	436	British Airways	G-CIVB	15.2.94
1019	27177	4B5	Korean Air	HL7490	17.2.94
1020	27175	467F	Cathay Pacific Airways	B-HUH	1.6.94
1021	25882	4J6	Air China	B-2445	25.2.94
1022	25812	436	British Airways	G-CIVC	26.2.94
1023	27217	412	Singapore Airlines	9V-SMY	17.3.94

Above: Line No 933 — Air New Zealand 747-419 ZK-NBU (c/n 25605) — was delivered on 14 September 1992, and is seen at London Heathrow in September 1998. *Nick Granger*

1024	26355	446	Japan Airlines	JA8910	19.3.94
1025	25703	4H6	Malaysian Airlines	9M-MPG	30.3.94
1026	26356	446	Japan Airlines	JA8911	30.3.94
1027	26055	458	El Al	4X-ELA	27.4.94
1028	24958	4Q8	Virgin Atlantic Airways	G-VFAB	28.4.94
1029	25705	4U3	Garuda Indonesian Airways	PK-GSH	27.5.94
1030	26549	412	Singapore Airlines	9V-SMZ	27.5.94
1031	27099	446	Japan Airlines	JA8912	31.5.94
1032	26056	458	El Al	4X-ELB	27.5.94
1033	27230	467	Cathay Pacific Airways	B-HUI	10.6.94
1034	27214	437	Air India	VT-ESP	28.6.94
1035	25780	48E	Asiana Airlines	HL7418	22.9.94
1036	26563	412F	Singapore Airlines	9V-SFA	5.8.94
1037	27341	4B5	Korean Air	HL7491	28.7.94
1038	27827	4F6	Canadian Airlines International	C-FGHZ	3.4.95
1039	27828	4F6	Philippine Airlines	N753PR	27.4.95
1040	26550	412	Singapore Airlines	9V-SPA	21.9.94
1041	27044	4H6	Malaysian Airlines	9M-MPH	22.9.94
1042	26561	412F	Singapore Airlines	9V-SFB	29.9.94
1043	26326	4Q8	Virgin Atlantic Airways	G-VHOT	12.10.94
1044	25781	48EF	Asiana Airlines	HL7419	4.11.94
1045	26551	412	Singapore Airlines	9V-SPB	28.10.94
1046	27338	469 Combi	Kuwait Airways	9K-ADE	29.11.94
1047	26610	4D7	Thai Airways International	HS-TGP	22.11.94
1048	27349	436	British Airways	G-CIVD	14.12.94
1049	27070	412	Singapore Airlines	9V-SPC	16.12.94
1050	27350	436	British Airways	G-CIVE	20.12.94
1051	27898	45E (SCD)	EVA Airways	B-18406	11.1.95
1052	26560	412F	Singapore Airlines	9V-SFC	14.2.95
1053	27899	45E (SCD)	EVA Airways	B-18407	22.2.95
1054	25883	4J6	Air China	B-2447	23.2.95
1055	26397	4B5	Korean Air	HL7492	23.2.95
1056	26552	412	Singapore Airlines	9V-SPD	30.3.95
1057	26398	4B5	Korean Air	HL7493	22.3.95

1058	25434	436	British Airways	G-CIVF	29.3.95
1059	25815	436	British Airways	G-CIVG	20.4.95
1060	27436	481D	All Nippon Airways	JA8965	28.4.95
1061	27595	467	Cathay Pacific Airways	B-HUJ	23.5.95
1062	27915	458	El Al	4X-ELC	31.5.95
1063	27965	409	Mandarin Airlines	B-16801	14.6.95
1064	25783	48EF	Asiana Airlines	HL7420	27.6.95
1065	27503	467F	Cathay Pacific Airways	B-HUK	12.7.95
1066	27442	481D	All Nippon Airways	JA8966	11.12.95
1067	27662	4B5	Korean Air	HL7494	10.8.95
1068	27663	469	Philippine Airlines	N754PR	29.3.96
1069	26553	412F	Singapore Airlines	9V-SFD	29.8.95
1070	26554	412	Singapore Airlines	9V-SPE	13.10.95
1071	27723	4D7	Thai Airways International	HS-TGR	7.11.95
1072	27071	412	Singapore Airlines	9V-SPF	4.12.95
1073	28096	4B5	Korean Air	HL7495	28.12.95
1074	26562	412	Singapore Airlines	9V-SPG	15.2.96
1075	26555	412	Singapore Airlines	9V-SPH	7.3.96
1076	28092	45E Combi	EVA Airways	N408EV	17.4.96
1077	28093	45E Combi	EVA Airways	N409EV	1.5.96
1078	25809	436	British Airways	G-CIVH	23.4.96
1079	25814	436	British Airways	G-CIVI	2.5.96
1080	28086	430	Lufthansa	D-ABVO	17.5.96
1081	26255	4Q8	Virgin Atlantic Airways	G-VBIG	10.6.96
1082	28022	412	Singapore Airlines	9V-SPI	20.6.96
1083	26400	4B5	Korean Air	HL7496	27.6.96
1084	26556	412	Singapore Airlines	9V-SPJ	17.7.96
1085	26890	422	United Airlines	N193UA	7.8.96
1086	25784	48E	Asiana Airlines	HL7421	16.8.96
1087	26401	4B5F	Korean Air	HL7497	6.9.96
1088	26892	422	United Airlines	N194UA	19.9.96
1089	28094	437	Air India	VT-EVA	31.10.96
1090	28195	406 Combi	KLM	PH-BFS	15.10.96
1091	27672	4H6	Malaysian Airlines	9M-MPI	25.10.96
1092	26402	4B5	Korean Air	HL7498	31.10.96
1093	28095	437	Air India	VT-EVB	15.11.96
1094	28263	412F	Singapore Airlines	9V-SFE	26.11.96
1095	26403	4B5	Korean Air	HL7472	26.11.96
1096	28367	48EF	Asiana Airlines	HL7422	18.12.96
1097	26616	4D7	Thai Airways International	HS-TGT	20.12.96
1098	28335	4B5	Korean Air	HL7473	23.12.96
1099	28023	412	Singapore Airlines	9V-SPK	21.1.97
1100	28194	4Q8	Virgin Atlantic Airways	G-VTOP	28.1.97
1101	26557	412	Singapore Airlines	9V-SPL	30.1.97
1102	25817	436	British Airways	G-CIVJ	11.2.97
1103	28284	430	Lufthansa	D-ABVP	25.2.97
1104	25818	436	British Airways	G-CIVK	28.2.97
1105	28026	412F	Singapore Airlines	9V-SFF	13.3.97
1106	28285	430	Lufthansa	D-ABVR	13.3.97
1107	26404	4B5	Korean Air	HL7460	26.3.97
1108	27478	436	British Airways	G-CIVL	28.3.97
1109	28286	430	Lufthansa	D-ABVS	18.4.97
1110	28287	430	Lufthansa	D-ABVT	28.4.97
1111	27724	4D7	Thai Airways International	HS-TGW	28.4.97
1112	28459	406 Combi	KLM	PH-BFT	15.5.97
1113	26899	422	United Airlines	N195UA	23.5.97
1114	28709	409	China Airlines	B-18201	29.5.97
1115	25782	48E Combi	Asiana Airlines	HL7423	30.5.97
1116	28700	436	British Airways	G-CIVM	5.6.97
1117	28757	41R	Virgin Atlantic Airways	G-VAST	17.6.97
1118	26405	4B5	Korean Air	HL7461	24.6.97

1119	28754	4J6 (SCD)	Air China	B-2467	30.6.97
1120	28715	422	United Airlines	N196UA	30.6.97
1121	26901	422	United Airlines	N197UA	21.7.97
1122	28339	468	Saudi Arabian Airlines	HZ-AIV	24.12.97
1123	26406	4B5F	Korean Air	HL7462	31.7.97
1124	28716	422	United Airlines	N198UA	20.8.97
1125	25868	4R7F	Cargolux	LX-KCV	26.8.97
1126	28717	422	United Airlines	N199UA	16.9.97
1127	28196	406 (SCD)	KLM	PH-BFU	8.9.97
1128	28755	4J6 Combi	Air China	B-2468	16.9.97
1129	28848	436	British Airways	G-CIVN	29.9.97
1130	28426	4H6	Malaysian Airlines	9M-MPJ	14.10.97
1131	28551	48E	Air Namibia	V5-NMA	21.10.99
1132	28710	409	China Airlines	B-18202	22.10.97
1133	28282	481	All Nippon Airways	JA401A	13.11.97
1134	27725	4D7	Thai Airways International	HS-TGX	12.11.97
1135	28849	436	British Airways	G-CIVO	5.12.97
1136	28711	409	China Airlines	B-18203	5.12.97
1137	28712	409	China Airlines	B-18205	18.12.97
1138	28340	468	Saudi Arabian Airlines	HZ-AIW	13.2.98
1139	29053	4R7F	Cargolux	LX-LCV	19.12.97
1140	29061	45E	EVA Airways	B-16410	19.1.98
1141	26902	422	United Airlines	N104UA	22.1.98
1142	28283	481	All Nippon Airways	JA402A	29.1.98
1143	29101	430	Lufthansa	D-ABVM	7.2.98
1144	28850	436	British Airways	G-CIVP	17.2.98
1145	29030	409	China Airlines	B-18206	25.2.98
1146	25820	436	British Airways	G-CIVR	2.3.98
1147	28427	4H6	Malaysian Airlines	9M-MPK	20.3.98
1148	28851	436	British Airways	G-CIVS	13.3.98
1149	25821	436	British Airways	G-CIVT	20.3.98
1150	28428	4H6	Malaysian Airlines	9M-MPL	30.3.98
1151	29111	45E	EVA Airways	B-16411	27.4.98
1152	28435	4H6	Malaysian Airlines	9M-MPM	14.4.98
1153	26359	445	Japan Airlines	JA8913	30.4.98
1154	25810	436	British Airways	G-CIVU	24.4.98
1155	26407	4B5	Korean Air	HL7402	30.12.98
1156	25819	436	British Airways	G-CIVV	22.5.98
1157	25822	436	British Airways	G-CIVW	15.5.98
1158	28959	4F6	South African Airways	ZS-SBK	30.12.98
1159	29112	45E	EVA Airways	B-16412	28.5.98
1160	28552	48E	Asiana Airlines	HL7428	18.6.99
1161	27602	4F6	Air New Zealand	ZK-SUJ	7.10.98
1162	28468	444	South African Airways	ZS-SAK	30.6.98
1163	26408	4B5F	Korean Air	HL7403	30.12.98
1164	28705	4D7	Thai Airways International	HS-TGY	22.12.98
1165	29252	47UF	Atlas Air	N491MC	29.7.98
1166	26360	446	Japan Airlines	JA8914	23.7.98
1167	28960	4F6	South African Airways	ZS-SBS	30.12.98
1168	26900	422	United Airlines	N107UA	20.8.98
1169	29253	47UF	Atlas Air	N492MC	12.8.98
1170	26409	4B5	Korean Air	HL7404	30.12.98
1171	26903	422	United Airlines	N108UA	28.8.98
1172	28852	436	British Airways	G-CIVX	3.9.98
1173	26558	412F	Singapore Airlines	9V-SFG	3.9.98
1174	28961	4F6	Abu Dhabi Amin Flight	A6-YAS	(awaited)
1175	28756	4J6	Air China	B-2469	28.9.98
1176	29219	409	China Airlines	B-18207	28.9.98
1177	29406	41R	Virgin Atlantic Airways	G-VXLG	30.9.98
1178	28853	436	British Airways	G-CIVY	29.9.98
1179	29254	47UF	Atlas Air	N493MC	21.10.98

1180	26910	419	Air New Zealand	ZK-NBV	31.10.98
1181	29070	4J6	Air China	B-2470	29.10.98
1182	28341	468	Saudi Arabian Airlines	HZ-AIX	18.11.98
1183	28854	436	British Airways	G-CIVZ	31.10.98
1184	29255	47UF	Atlas Air	N494MC	4.12.98
1185	26906	422	United Airlines	N109UA	16.11.98
1186	29031	409	China Airlines	B-18208	20.11.98
1187	29119	444	South African Airways	ZS-SAZ	30.11.98
1188	26361	446	Japan Airlines	JA8915	30.11.98
1189	29729	4R7F	Cargolux	LX-MCV	8.12.98
1190	28855	436	British Airways	G-BYGA	14.12.98
1191	29492	430	Lufthansa	D-ABVU	21.12.98
1192	29261	47UF	Atlas Air	N408MC	15.12.98
1193	26908	422	United Airlines	N116UA	29.12.98
1194	28856	436	British Airways	G-BYGB	17.1.99
1195	25823	436	British Airways	G-BYGC	19.1.99
1196	28857	436	British Airways	G-BYGD	26.1.99
1197	28810	422	United Airlines	N117UA	29.1.99
1198	28858	436	British Airways	G-BYGE	5.2.99
1199	29262	481	All Nippon Airways	JA403A	25.2.99
1200	25824	436	British Airways	G-BYGF	17.2.99
1201	28811	422	United Airlines	N118UA	24.2.99
1202	26362	446	Japan Airlines	JA8916	18.3.99
1203	29730	4R7F	Cargolux	LX-NCV	3.3.99
1204	29263	481	All Nippon Airways	JA404A	30.3.99
1205	29493	430	Lufthansa	D-ABVW	13.3.99
1206	26477	451	Northwest Airlines	N671US	29.3.99
1207	28812	422	United Airlines	N119UA	29.3.99
1208	29899	446	Japan Airlines	JA8917	20.4.99
1209	29166	422	United Airlines	N120UA	12.4.99
1210	27603	48EF	Asiana Airlines	HL7426	14.4.99
1211	29167	422	United Airlines	N121UA	22.4.99
1212	28859	436	British Airways	G-BYGG	29.4.99
1213	29256	47UF	Atlas Air/BA World Cargo	N495MC	26.4.99
1214	28706	4D7	Thai Airways International	HS-TGZ	11.5.99
1215	29328	458	El Al	4X-ELD	24.5.99
1216	28342	468	Saudi Arabian Airlines	HZ-AIY	9.12.99
1217	29257	47UF	Atlas Air	N496MC	30.6.99
1218	29168	422	United Airlines	N122UA	14.6.99
1219	29906	409	China Airlines	B-18209	25.6.99
1220	29258	47UF	Atlas Air/China Airlines	N497MC	15.7.99
1221	28813	422	United Airlines	N127UA	2.8.99
1222	29731	4R7F	Cargolux	LX-OCV	12.7.99
1223	30267	451	Northwest Airlines	N672US	19.7.99
1224	28032	412F	Singapore Airlines	9V-SFH	5.8.99
1225	28460	406 Combi	KLM	PH-BFV	16.8.99
1226	30268	451	Northwest Airlines	N673US	24.8.99
1227	29259	47UF	Atlas Air/China Airlines	N498MC	26.8.99
1228	29376	419	Air New Zealand	ZK-NBW	8.9.99
1229	29071	4J6	China Airlines	B-2471	22.9.99
1230	25564	438	QANTAS	VH-OJS	30.9.99
1231	29732	4R7F	Cargolux	LX-PCV	29.9.99
1232	30269	451	Northwest Airlines	N674US	18.10.99
1233	25565	438	QANTAS	VH-OJT	26.10.99
1234	27650	446	Japan Airlines	JA8918	21.11.99
1235	30400	4R7F	Cargolux	LX-RCV	23.11.99
1236	27100	446	Japan Airlines	JA8919	16.12.99
1237	29868	430	Lufthansa	D-ABVX	22.12.99
1238	30201	4G4F	USAF AL1	00-0001	21.1.00
1239	25566	438	QANTAS	VH-OJU	24.1.00
1240	29260	47UF	Atlas Air	N499MC	17.2.00